Mrs. T.D. Crewdson

Lays of the Reformation

And other lyrics scriptural and miscellaneous

Mrs. T.D. Crewdson

Lays of the Reformation

And other lyrics scriptural and miscellaneous

ISBN/EAN: 9783744797221

Printed in Europe, USA, Canada, Australia, Japan

Cover: Foto ©Thomas Meinert / pixelio.de

More available books at **www.hansebooks.com**

CONTENTS.

Lays of the Reformation.

	PAGE
MORNING STARS, PART I.	3
PART II.	11
PART III.	19
NOTES	29
THE SCHLOSS-KIRCHE DOOR	35
LUTHER AT WORMS	49
NOTES	72
LAY OF THE WARTBURG	79
NOTES	91
THE HERMIT OF LIVRY, PART I.	94
PART II.	101
PART III.	108

Scripture Lyrics.

THE BOY OF LYSTRA, PART I.	117
PART II.	123
PART III.	129

CONTENTS.

	PAGE
THE BROTHERS	136
"WARNED OF GOD"	146
AN ARK SONG	151
A VOYAGE FROM TROAS TO NEAPOLIS, A.D. 53	153
NOTES	162
A SABBATH MORN AT PHILIPPI	164
JEPHTHAH'S DAUGHTER	170
ELIEZER AT THE FOUNTAIN	182
THE BETTER CHOICE — MOAB OR ISRAEL?	190
THE GLEANER	195
THE LITTLE CAPTIVE MAID	200

Miscellaneous.

RUNNYMEDE	215
PHILIPPINA WELSER	226
A GOOD-FRIDAY LEGEND	235
AN OLD VERGER'S TALE	246
CHIMINGS	252
TO CECILIA	255
THE BABE AND THE SAINT	259
A SABBATH REMINISCENCE	265
OUR DEPARTED TWAIN	268
TO MARY	275
MY GRANDMOTHER'S WALKING-CANE	278
HYMN — "I WILL BLESS THE LORD AT ALL TIMES"	283

LAYS OF THE REFORMATION.

B

" WHEN I recall to mind how the bright and blissful Reformation (by Divine power) struck through the black and settled night of ignorance and antichristian tyranny, methinks a sovereign and reviving joy must needs rush into the bosom of him that reads or hears; and the sweet odour of the returning Gospel embathe his soul with the fragrancy of heaven. Then was the sacred Bible sought out of the dusty corners where profane falsehood and neglect had thrown it; the schools opened; divine and human learning raked out of forgotten tongues; the princes and critics trooping apace to the new-erected banner of salvation; the martyrs, with the unresistible might of weakness, shaking the powers of darkness and scorning the fiery rage of the old red dragon."—MILTON.

MORNING STARS.

PART I.

> . . . . "He made the stars,
> And set them in the firmament of heaven
> To illuminate the earth, and rule the day
> In their vicissitude, and rule the night,
> And light from darkness to divide."
> MILTON, *Paradise Lost*, Book 7th.

Now count five hundred rings, or more,
   In the bole of the old oak-trees
That wave their broken shadows o'er
   The rocky banks of Tees;
And bid the chronicles of yore
   Bring back five centuries.

In Egglestone old Priory [1]
    The lamps are burning dim,
And daylight, with a gentle eye,
    Peeps through the windows trim;
And the monks are chaunting drowsily
    The sweet old matin hymn.

They chaunt it bravely, note by note,
    Though half asleep they seem;
For they know it every word by rote,
    And could sing it in a dream:
And o'er their pauses softly float
    The voices of the stream.

Betwixt the sculptured traceries
    The tender light is stealing;
Pouring the quiet of the skies,—
    Like some fresh breath of healing,—
Across the missals' glowing dyes,
    And o'er those figures kneeling.

Down o'er the Abbot's broidered gown
    It sheds a chastening ray;
And on the poor monk's shaven crown,
    And coat of hodden grey;
And o'er the altar trickles down,
    Like blessing dropped astray.

There sits a gentle lady fair,—
    In ancient hall sits she,—
In kirtle edged with miniver,
    And coat of cramoisie:
And a little babe, of beauty rare,
    Is sleeping on her knee.²

You might search each Yorkshire dale anear,
    And search afar each wold,
Yet never find that infant's peer,
    So beauteous to behold!
With lambent eye and forehead clear,
    And hair like thredded gold.

The morning star, so pale and mild,
   Through the old lattice crept,
And shone upon the dreaming child,
   The while he softly slept;
And the young babe awoke, and smiled,
   As o'er his lip it swept.

The Lady spake out merrily,—
   "Alack, my pretty son!
The star of morn seems claiming thee,[3]
   In earnest, for her own;
And o'er thy forehead, stealthily,
   Her holy chrism thrown."

Time flew. The babe at Wycliffe hall[4]
   Like lily, grew apace:
A gentle Boy—the loved of all—
   With sweet, angelic face;
And a shrewd fancy, held in thrall
   By tender cords of grace.

There sat a grandeur on his brow,
    So pure and undefiled,
Which even made the aged bow
    In reverence to the child.
And now and then there flushed a glow
    Of transport when he smiled.

And day by day this little one
    Hied o'er the craggy hill,
By river side, through forest lone,
    And by the splashing gill;
That the poor monks at Egglestone
    Might learn him clerkly skill.

Like a pure dewdrop from the sky,
    On scenes of gloom and din;
Or like a sun-ray from on high,
    This gentle youth dropped in;
With low, sweet voice, and guileless eye,
    Reproving sloth and sin.

The aged faces grew less old,
    Scanning his youthful grace;
The cynic less morose and cold,
    While gazing on his face;
Less confident the coarse and bold,
    And less depraved the base.

That old monk, with the artist eye,
    And open manuscript,
And glowing palette—patiently
    Waits—with his pencil dipped,
Until the saintly boy draw nigh
    The old "Scriptorium" crypt.

With brush 'twixt finger and 'twixt thumb,
    And gilded vellum spread,
He waits until his model come
    For the young Baptist's head:
Impatient lest the morning bloom
    From the boy's cheek be fled.

It was but little they could teach,
    Beyond their missal's store;
But this was written in the speech
    The grand old Vulgate bore;
And Latin words were steps to reach
    A higher, holier lore.

" Now, read me not about your saints,
    But take this volume down,
Which tells how Christ was railed against,
    And wore the thorny crown;
And how the Lord of glory faints
    Upon the cross—alone!

" And read me how the Baptist felt,
    When first the Christ he knew;
And how he gladly would have knelt
    To loose his Master's shoe;
And how he wore the rough hair-belt
    O'er loyal heart and true!

"How Jesus raised the ruler's dead,
 And the poor widow's son;
And how the multitude were fed
 With food, where there was none.
For when God's children cry for bread,
 He doth not give a stone."

The lazy Friars—not a few—
 Swore, by Saint Peter's rood,
That little JOHN DE WYCLIFFE grew
 Too clerkly and too shrewd!
"And some," quoth they, "will live to rue
 This child—so over-good!"

MORNING STARS.

PART II.

" . . . . The morning star of song, who made
   His music heard below;
Dan Chaucer, the first warbler, whose sweet breath
   Preluded those melodious bursts that fill
The spacious times of great Elizabeth
   With sounds that echo still."— TENNYSON.

Two moving shadows slowly glide

   Forth from the sylvan shade!

Two youths are pacing, side by side,

   Up Thorsgill's broomy glade!

The woodland creatures scarcely hide —

   The shy are scarce afraid.

Two pleasant voices, young and free,
    In earnest converse blend ;
Yet neither seemeth to agree,
    In counsel, with his friend ;
And though they commune courteously,
    They neither yield nor bend.

The accent of the younger shames
    The northman's simple tongue ;
It smatters of the banks of Thames,
    And of the joust and song ;
And of the courtly London dames,
    The dance, and festive throng.

He wears a camlet rochet grand,
    Broider'd with golden thread—
A jewell'd ring on dainty hand,
    And pointed hosen red ;
And a jaunty cap, with plume and band,
    Placed sidewise on his head ;—

A merry youth!—And yet, o'er all,
    The soul immortal glanced;
And genius spurned at fashion's thrall,
    And loved the Muses' haunts.
And on those lips, refined and small,
And eyes like Amadis' of Gaul,
    The soul of song lay tranced.

He had quaff'd largely at the well
    Of sweet Provençal lore;
And just had found a hollow shell
    Upon his native shore:—
And almost started at the swell
    Of song which floated o'er!

Quoth he, "Dear WYCLIFFE! those are wise,
    And I a frolic youth;
Yet both hate falsehood and disguise,
    And both revere the truth:[5]
Thou, a true saint, with those pure eyes,
    And I—no saint, forsooth!

" Oh, I would sweep my country's lyre,
    With daring hand and free,
And tune to song each stubborn wire,
    Till men shall say of me,
' DAN CHAUCER is the princely sire
    Of England's poesy!'

" Ah, I will such, like honey-bee,
    The flowers of fair Provence;
And steal, from Guillaume de Lorris,
    The Rose's quaint romance;[6]
And sip my pipe of Malvoisie
    In Windsor's royal haunts.

" I'll pledge thy health in jewell'd cup,
    Thou saintly Gospeler!
When Percy and when Chaucer sup
    With noble Lancaster.[7]
Ah, those old monks!—we'll show them up,
    And lash each lazy *frère*."

He laughed a jocund peal;—it rung
  Adown the forest glen;
The woodpecker, with flippant tongue,
  Laughed merrily again;
The heron from the river sprung,
  The bittern from the fen.

" Alas, Sir Bard! Thy stinging dart
  May scar the Dragon's skin;
But will not reach the evil heart,
  Nor mend the life within.
He'll writhe a moment at the smart,
  But only hug the sin.

" 'Tis not thy laugh —'tis not my sigh—
  Nor frolic jest—nor frown—
Can Antichrist, in strength, defy,
  And smite his banner down:
The Saviour must be lifted high,
  Ere Sin be overthrown.

" God give me grace!—I will not grant
    Sloth to my labouring breast
Until His Ark of Covenant
    Shall find a place of rest;
And England's hills and dales shall pant
    For blessings—*and be bless'd.*

" I'll open wide a living brook
    On every barren moor;
I'll take the Gospel's holy book,
    And give it to the poor;
And blind men on the light shall look,
    And, seeing Christ, adore!

" From where the Loire in sunshine flows
    Thou bring'st the quaint '*Romaunt;*'
And of the worldling's vapid woes,
    Dear Bard! thou lov'st to chaunt:
But *I* would pluck sweet Sharon's Rose,
And wheresoe'er the poor man goes
    That fragrant flower I'd plant.

"I'd pour soft drops of Gilead's balm
  O'er every wounded head;
I'd wave the victor's holy palm
  O'er every dying bed;
And laud, and prayer, and dulcet psalm,
The troubled soul shall cheer and calm,
  In native language read."

"Forsooth!— Thy saintship's reveries
  My poet-dreams outshine!
But, ah! I'd creep on bended knees
  To old Saint Becket's shrine;
And I would scatter to the breeze
The choicest pearls of Indian seas—
Aye, give my sweetest melodies—
  For one such dream as thine!"

They part.— Life's river soon shall fret
  And brawl betwixt the twain,

And many a sun of hope shall set,
And many a star shall wane;
And laurel wreaths with tears be wet,
Ere clasp they hands again!

MORNING STARS.

PART III.

"Our Wycliffe's preaching was the lamp at which all the succeeding reformers lighted their tapers."— MILTON.

A SINGLE horseman, from a lane,
   Is ambling into sight!—
With jewell'd hand he checks the rein
   Of palfrey, sleek and white,
To listen to the merle's refrain,
Until those troubled eyes again
   O'erflow with frolic light.

The palfrey crops the linden spray,
  Dripping with dews of eve.
The rider's fingers softly play
  With threads of thought—to weave
A dewy stanza, in a lay,
  About a "Flower and Leaf!"[8]

Time hath pass'd roughly, with his plough,
  Across that face of care,
And grooved deep furrows on the brow,
  Still grand with genius rare;
As if the envied laurel bough
  Distill'd but poison there!

Anon, the curfew's mellow chime
  Floats from an old church-tower—
The poet drops his threaded rhyme
  About the Leaf and Flower;
And, chafing at the waste of time,
  Leaves fancy's dewy bower.

The sweet "Amen" seem'd lingering still
    Around the house of prayer—
The breath of praise seem'd yet to fill
    The balmy, sunset air—
As, o'er the brook and up the hill,
    The scatter'd people fare.

The poet wondered to behold
    The light of gentle grace,
Which shone, as from a lamp of gold,
    On every peasant's face:
A look of holy peace, that told
The flock had found the shepherd's fold,
    A quiet resting-place!

The halt and aged seemed to lean
    Upon some secret stay;
The heavy-laden to have seen
    Their burden rolled away;
The solaced mourner to have been
    Where she could weep and pray.

Like picture of some saint of yore,
    In Gothic niche portrayed,
The preacher, from the low-arched door,
    Emerges from the shade:
While sunset glories, floating o'er,
A golden nimbus, softly pour
    Around his snow-white head.

Like pilgrims met at eventide
    To pitch the desert tent;
Like aged brothers, parted wide,
    To meet when day is spent;
The friends are seated, side by side,
    In converse eloquent.[9]

"WYCLIFFE! How soft the shadows lay
    Beneath those summer trees,
When we twain dreamed our dreams one day,
    Beside the banks of Tees!

E'en as that stream, in reckless play,

Tossed to the winds its foamy spray,

So have I tossed life's wine away,

    And sucked the bitter lees.

" Though kings have twined my laureate wreath,

    And warriors sung my praise;

Though time hath breathed immortal breath

    Upon my deathless lays;

And princes crouched to bask beneath

    The sparkle of my rays;

" 'Twas only while my merry jest

    Could brim the festal bowl,

And while my witty laugh gave zest

    To the dull worldling's *rôle*,

That CHAUCER's jewelled baldrick pressed

    Across this troubled soul.

" 'Twas all a dream! Life's only truth
    Was once,— in stormy fight,
When stood the friend of Geoffrey's youth,
    Braving the crozier's might;
And the court-poet, bland and smooth,
Defied man's threat, and scorned his ruth,
    And stood by WYCLIFFE's right.[10]

" The dream was o'er! I woke at last
    To find the laurel crown
Shiv'ring in autumn's stormy blast,
    Blighted, and sere, and brown;
And from my lute — mine idol — passed
    The glory and renown.

" Like a tired child, come home at night,
    With lagging, faltering tread;
(His hollow reed in tuneless plight,
    His flowers all dank and dead,)
I come to borrow of thy light,
    To find my way to bed!"

Ah! who shall tell what holy cheer
    Came down, like summer rain?
How heavenly love cast out earth's fear,
    With all its shadowy train?
And how the Lord of grace drew near,
    And talkèd with the twain?

Like travellers who appoint a tryst,
    Before they part in love,
Minded to meet again in Christ,
    Within the courts above,
The Poet and Evangelist
    On severed pathways move.

Time passed. The gales of midnight sigh
    Among the churchyard trees:
The wailing streamlet murmurs by,
    Tost by the gusty breeze;
And Seraph-hosts are drawing nigh,
To hail, with " Alleluias" high,
    The fettered saint's release.

Ah! if men's eyes were finely skilled
   To scan immortal things,
They'd see his dying chamber filled
   With angels' radiant wings;
And if their plaintive sighs were stilled,
Perchance the ear of faith were thrilled
   With sounds from viewless strings.

Time passed. The trysting-place drew near,
   The holy tryst was kept:
And princes thronged around the bier
   Where England's Poet slept;
And strangers came to drop a tear,
   And merrie England wept.

They scooped their minstrel's narrow grave
   Among the royal dead;
And the banners of the mighty wave
   Around his laureled head;
And the scutcheons of the proud and brave
   Glow round his dreamless bed.

The Poet left to earth,—" a well
    Of English undefiled :"[11]
A place to gather asphodel
    For every minstrel child!
Alas! that e'er its babblings tell,
Of baneful flower and noxious bell,
    And gropings through a wild.

Each left his legacy. The saint
    Left glorious wealth untold,
More than the mind of man can paint,
    And more than eyes behold:
To poor—and lone—and sick—and faint,
    Pearls—silver—finest gold!

He opened wide a living brook
    By cot and cabin door;
He made the Gospel's holy Book
    Speak peace from shore to shore;
The bread of life from Christ he took,
    And gave it to the poor.

He lit Truth's lamp, at dead of night,
    With patient toil and skill;
He bore it bravely through the fight,
    And set it on a hill.
And distant watchers hailed the sight,
And lit their torch at WYCLIFFE's light,
    —And, lo! it burneth still![12]

NOTES.

Note 1, page 4.

"In Egglestone old Priory."

The ruins of Egglestone Priory, or Abbey (for Tanner calls it the latter and Leland the former), are beautifully situated upon the angle formed by a little dell called Thorsgill, at its junction with the river Tees. The Priory is supposed to have been founded about the end of the reign of Henry the Second.

Note 2, page 5.

"And a little babe, of beauty rare,
Is sleeping on her knee."

Most of the portraits professing to be likenesses of Wycliffe indicate a high style of beauty, both in feature and in expression. Probably not one is an original likeness: but in the portraits of celebrated men there has generally been some remote, historical picture, or description, from which copyists have originally worked.

NOTE 3, page 6.

"The star of morn seems claiming thee."

About the same transition-period from darkness to daylight, arose England's two Morning Stars. In 1324 was born John Wycliffe, in an obscure Yorkshire valley on the banks of the Tees. In 1326 was born Geoffrey Chaucer, on the banks of the Thames. Both were "*Morning Stars.*" The one ushered in the dawn of religious reformation and liberty of conscience, the other was the father of English poetry. To compare the heavenly vocation of the former with the intellectual services of the latter would seem folly, excepting in so far as they both contended (though with very different weapons) for truth, and both for the unmasking of falsehood. Moreover, they both contributed to settle and fix the noble language of their native land, then capriciously fluctuating between the Norman-French and the Anglicised Saxon. Wycliffe, by his translation of the Bible into fine old Saxon-English, gave to the common people the Word of Truth in the language of hearth and home. Chaucer, by his courtly diction, drawn from the polished South as well as from the sterner North, imparted just that richness and flexibility which were needed to commend his native tongue to the peer as well as to the peasant, and to prove its adaptation for general literature.

NOTE 4, page 6.

"Time flew. The babe at Wycliffe hall."

Dr. Whittaker, in his *History of Richmondshire*, painfully disputes the general impression respecting the place of Wycliffe's birth. His arguments, however, scarcely unsettle the current opinion; namely, that the great Forerunner of the Protestant Reformation was born at *Wycliffe Hall*, on the banks of the Tees, near Barnard Castle.

NOTE 5, page 13.

" Yet both hate falsehood and disguise,
And both revere the truth."

That the Poet sympathised with the Gospel Doctor in many of his enlightened religious opinions is an historical fact.

NOTE 6, page 14.

" And steal, from Guillaume de Lorris,
The Rose's quaint romance."

The celebrated old poem called *The Romaunt of the Rose* was translated by Chaucer into English metre, from the old French of Guillaume de Lorris.

NOTE 7, page 14.

" I'll pledge thy health in jewell'd cup,
Thou saintly Gospeler!
When Percy and when Chaucer sup
With noble Lancaster."

John of Gaunt, the princely Duke of Lancaster, was the patron of the Poet as well as the protector of the Reformer; and Chaucer heartily entered into the Duke's espousal of Wycliffe's cause.

Note 8, page 20.

"A dewy stanza, in a lay,
About a '*Flower and Leaf.*'"

See Chaucer's Poems. The fable of "the Flower and the Leaf" is an exquisite thing—fresh and dewy.

Note 9, page 22.

"The friends are seated, side by side,
In converse eloquent."

That there really existed a personal friendship betwixt the twain (in other words, that the "Morning Stars" sometimes loved to sing together) may be further guessed by Chaucer's lovely description of a true Gospel Minister of his times, said to be a portrait, from the life, of the Rector of Lutterworth. The features are limned in with such a loving hand, that it seems impossible to doubt their truthfulness.

"A good man of religion did I see,
And a poor parson of a town was he:
But rich he was of holy thought and work,
And also was a learned man—a clerk,
And truly would Christ's holy gospel preach,
And his parishioners devoutly teach.
Benign he was, and wondrous diligent,
And patient when adversity was sent.
　　*　　*　　*　　*　　*
Wide was his parish—houses far asunder—
But he neglected nought for rain or thunder.

> In sickness and in grief to visit all,
> The farthest in his parish, great and small;
> Always on foot, and in his hand a stave.
>
>   *   *   *   *   *
>
> And though he holy was, and virtuous,
> He was to sinful men full piteous.
> His words were strong, but not with anger fraught;
> A love benignant he distinctly taught.
> To draw mankind to heaven by gentleness
> And good example, was his business.
> But if that any one were obstinate,
> Whether he were of high or low estate;
> Him would he sharply check with altered mien;
> A better parson there was no where seen.
> He paid no court to pomps or reverence,
> Nor spiced his conscience at his soul's expence;
> But Jesu's love, which owns no pride or pelf,
> He taught,—*but first he followed it himself.*"

Note 10, page 24.

> "'Twas all a dream! Life's only truth
>   Was once,—in stormy fight,
> When stood the friend of Geoffrey's youth,
>   Braving the crozier's might;
> And the court-poet, bland and smooth,
> Defied man's threat, and scorned his ruth,
>   And stood by WYCLIFFE's right."

There is an interesting historical picture by Egan, engraved by Jones, in which is represented the citation of Wycliffe (in Saint Paul's) to answer the charge of heresy.

Geoffrey Chaucer's poet-face may be seen in close proximity to the beautiful countenance of the Rector of Lutterworth.

Note 11, page 27.

" The Poet left to earth,—' a well
Of English undefiled.' "

" Dan Chaucer! well of English undefiled."—Spenser.

Note 12, page 28.

" He lit Truth's lamp, at dead of night,
With patient toil and skill;
He bore it bravely through the fight,
And set it on a hill.
And distant watchers hailed the sight,
And lit their torch at Wycliffe's light,
—And, lo! it burneth still!"

Milton, in one of his prose essays, truly remarks, " Our Wycliffe's preaching was the lamp at which all the succeeding reformers lighted their tapers."

The lamp never went out. It shone across the sea to the continent of Europe; and was welcomed with a response from Alpine fastnesses and Bohemian forests. 'Till, at length, the great Saxon Reformer awoke, and, with his powerful voice, proclaimed the daylight.

THE SCHLOSS-KIRCHE DOOR.

(AN OLD MONK'S TALE.)

Luther affixed his celebrated Theses to the door of the old Schloss-Kirche at Wittenberg, on the eve of All Saints' Day, 1517.

" THE Seller of Indulgences,
 With all his pampered band,
Had trafficked with his deadly ware
 Throughout the Saxon's land ;—
The Saxon's land, where towers are strong,
 And wills and deeds are bold ;
And honest hearts shall never be
Turned by the wards of any key,
 Of iron or of gold !

"The Seller of Indulgences
  Was worthy of his craft;
He took away the people's gold,
  And left the poison-draught.
He took away the people's wealth
  To gild Saint Peter's dome,
But left a shaft with force unspent,
Whose pointed barb should back be sent—
  By a strong arm—to Rome!

" 'Twas not the soft and jewelled hand
  Of Kaiser or of King,
Which laid the arrow on the bow,
  And pulled the whirring string.
'Twas not a hand in glove of steel
  Made strong by sturdy fight;
Nor yet the pale and sinewy hand
That wields the gilded crozier-wand,
  With proud, yet borrowed might.

" It was an arm well nerved for fight,
    And strong to will and dare —
A poor monk's feeble hand, made strong
    By lifting up in prayer!
By drawing down its secret might
    From treasuries unfailing;
Wrestling, like Jacob, all night long,
Halting and weak, while waxing strong,
    And, as a prince, prevailing!*

" He rose up from his knees one eve —
    (Methinks I see him now,
With autumn's stormy twilight poured
    Upon his massive brow) —
Dashed down his book of popish prayers,
    Recoiling with a start:
And, with a loving grasp, then took
Another and a holier Book,
    And girt it on his heart.

       * Genesis, xxxii. 28.

" I marked a sparkle of the eye,
    A freedom in each move,
Like what I've seen in champion knight
    When he throws down his glove.
The miner's son might match the knight,
    In gesture and in tone :
I know not how, but so it was,
The poor Augustine monk might pass
    For a highborn baron's son.

" Ah me ! No knight with plume and lance,
    E'er played a sterner *rôle!*
His morion was the convent cowl,
    His glove a written scroll—
A scroll whose every line was writ
    Mid sighs, and tears, and prayer :
And midnight's shade, and twilight's gleam,
And noontide's clear, unwavering beam,
    All left their pathway there.

" Along the convent corridor
    He strode, with steady pace —
The Brothers peeping from their cells
    To gaze upon his face.
And some did frown a scowl that well
    Might all heaven's saints dishearten:
But others raised their drooping head,
And wrung his hand, and whispering said,
    ' Christ bless thee, *Brother Martin!*'

" And then adown the old oak stairs,
    With muffled sandal shod,
He passed — and every ancient board
    Creaked harshly as he trod.
And out into the cloistered court,
    And 'neath the portal low;
And there the shades seemed backward driven,
And the pure, liquid light of heaven
    Streamed right upon his brow.

" Alone he trod the gabled street,
　　For men took little heed,
As yet, of what was Gospel truth,
　　And what the Romish creed.
Ithuriel had not touched the foe,
　　As yet, with fiery spear;
And made him shift his old disguise,
And starting from his lair, arise
　　In sin's true character.

" October's stormy evening sky
　　Lit up the old Schloss-Kirk,
And threw a crimson gleam adown
　　The stony tracery-work;
Pouring a broken ray aslant
　　Across the dusky aisle:
And, in the western portal dim,
Making the demon-masks look grim,
　　And stony saints to smile.

" He stood beneath the heavy arch,
   In the full ruddy light ;
And with his left hand grasped a nail,—
   A hammer with his right :—
Unrolled that scroll he writ with tears,
   And signed midst heaving groans :—
Rapp, rapp !—oh, door of Saxon oak !
Didst ever quail with such a stroke,
E'er since the woodman's hatchet woke
   The echoes with thy moans ?

" I shuddered as the vaulted aisle
   Gave back the hollow sound ;
And every shrine obeyed the sign,
   And sent the echo round.
Rapp, rapp !—a second nail is driven,
   Too firm for storms to move !
Rapp, rapp !—a third !—a fourth !—all right !
Hurrah for Europe's champion-knight !
   He hath thrown down the glove !

" When convent-chapel lamps were lit
    That eve, for vesper prayer,
No sweet voice chaunted forth the psalm
    So strong as his, so rare!
'Twould seem as if the burdened soul
    Had brought her weary load
Of hopes and fears, of gain and loss,
And Faith had nailed *all* to the cross,
    And left it there with God.

" The winter sun uprose next morn,
    Cold, cloudless, and serene;
Smiling a silvery smile of peace
    Across the frosty scene.
The old Schloss-Kirk, in festal pomp,
    Soon oped her portals wide;
And lines of priests, in grand array,
Spread out the relics for display,
To edify, on 'All Saints' Day,'
    The neighbouring country side.

" From many a hamlet's quiet shade,
    From many a storm-rent tower,
From forest path, and river's brink,
    And peaceful vintage bower;
On slow-paced mule, on prancing steed,
    On holy pilgrim staff,
They throng the gates, within, without,
And make the old walls ring with shout,
    And song, and psalm, and laugh.

" But song, and psalm, and laughter-shout
    Are changed for grave debate,
Soon as that giddy multitude
    Have reached the old Kirk-gate,
And spy those *Theses*, lettered out
    Clear, legible, and strong.
The clerkly con them o'er and o'er,
The learnèd read them to the poor,
And, halting round the grey Kirk-door,
    Cluster the gathering throng.

"The baron smiled a puzzled smile;
　　His lady laughed outright—
For woman's heart is always quick
　　To catch a ray of light.
The friars shook their shaven crowns—
　'The monk is mad,' quoth one—
But others sighed, 'If *he* be mad,
Augustine the like mania had,
　　And Paul, and sweet Saint John!'

"A pilgrim smote upon his breast,—
　'I might have prayed at home,
Nor dragged my weary, heavy heart,
　　And bleeding feet, to Rome!'
'Alack!' responds a burgher's dame,
　　Betwixt a smile and scowl,—
'I might have kept (and been no worse)
Those golden guelders in my purse,
Nor heaped, perchance, another curse
　　Upon poor Tetzel's soul.'

" But, ah! the smile of radiant joy
    Which lit the poor man's eye!
' Is there indulgence, then, for *me*
    Who have no gold to buy?
They told me that my lost one lies
    In purgatorial flame,
Because I had no coin, alas!
To buy a single priestly mass,
    To save my one ewe lamb.'

" In vain the swinging censer's breath
    Perfumes the heavy air;
And round the altar's glittering height
    A hundred tapers glare.
In vain the choral anthem swells,
    Their truant hearts to win;
And pompous sacristans in vain
Sweep the long aisle with rustling train,
    To lure the people in.

"Still, still around the old Kirk-door,
   In loud debate they stand—
The posies for the Virgin's shrine
   Slow withering in their hand.
That morn one strong electric shock
   Hath touched a thousand strings—
That morn the deathless soul awoke,
And started from beneath man's yoke
   To find that she hath wings!

"Ah me! Full many a year hath flown,
   And many a tempest's stroke
Hath struck, and back recoiled again
   From that old door of oak:
Yet, though an old man's eyes wax dim,
   And memory halts and fails,
And ears grow dull, methinks I hear,
In strong distinctness, bold and clear,
   That hammer on those nails.

" O'er vale and hill, o'er mount and plain,
    The booming echoes roll,
Knocking against the dungeon doors
    Of man's imprisoned soul.
The dark pine-forests caught the sound,
    The hills replied again;
The mountains sped it on its flight,
And tossed it on from height to height,
    And rolled it to the plain.

" Old Tyber frets his tawny wave,
    And chafes with muddy foam,
To speed the Vandal note of war
    On to the gates of Rome.
The seven hills awake from sleep,
    Affrighted at the peal;
And turning fiercely at the sound,
Old Antichrist receives a wound
    Which never more shall heal.

"Long since, I left my convent cell,
  For Christ, who made me free;
To preach His gospel to the poor,
  In glorious liberty;
To pray the spirit-prayer of faith
  Without the senseless beads;
To grasp the living Word of Light,
In all its quickening truth and might,
  Without man's deadening creeds.

"Ah! I can think on Him who bled
  Upon th' accursed tree,
Without the graven crucifix
  To help my memory.
Without the mass-book I can laud
  His grace, on bended knees;
And when my spirit plumes her wing,
Without my missal I can sing
  Sweet '*Benedicites!*'"

LUTHER AT WORMS,

IN 1521.

> " Ein feste Burg ist unser Gott,
> Ein gute Wehr und Waffen,
> Er helft uns frei aus aller Noth
> Die uns je hat betroffen."
>
> LUTHER.

THUS spake a youthful warrior,
   In the knightly days of old,—
With mirthful eye, and open brow,
   And step erect and bold :—
" Sit here, and tell me, grandsire,
   Some tale of daring deed ;
Of hero, girt with charmèd sword,
   Bridling his fiery steed !

Tell of the scaly dragon,[1]
    'Neath Siegfred's mighty hand —
The glory and the darling of
    The German's Fatherland!
How with a thousand plaudits,
    The dark pine-forests rang,
And ancient minstrels wove the lays
    Which fair young maidens sang."

The old man paused — high visions
    Upon his soul throng fast;
And memory's touch is wandering o'er
    The key-notes of the Past.
And when he spake, sonorous
    Became his voice, and clear —
Unlike the weak and faltering tones
    The youth was wont to hear.

"I'll tell thee of a hero,
    Before whose pure renown,

Down to the dust falls each sere leaf
    From Siegfred's lordly crown!
I'll tell thee of a braver
    Than all whose knightly praise
Is registered in chronicle,
    Or chaunted forth in lays.
Aye, boy! the *free soul's* champion!
    Who wielded such a brand,
As dauntless Siegfred never grasped
    Within his steel-gloved hand;
And dealt the old Arch-dragon
    A blow—so sturdily!—
That a thousand, thousand captive souls
    Were from his coil set free.

" It was a spring-tide morning?—
    I mind me how the vine
Was putting forth her tender leaves,
    Along the winding Rhine;

And how the silvery blossoms
    Were budding on the thorn;
And sprouted on the upland slopes,
    The young blades of the corn.

"But the peasant left his vineyard,
    And the lady left her bower,
And the baron, on his stout roan steed,
    Spurred down from castled tower;
And the smith forsook his anvil,
    And boys forgot their play,
To throng this old imperial town
    Upon that wondrous day.

"Ah me! I was a stripling;
    And my father's vassals said
That chestnut ringlets never waved
    Upon a comelier head;
And that the broidered doublet
    Ne'er spanned a nobler chest;

And that a fleeter step ne'er chased
    The leveret from her nest.

"I went forth on that morning
    A child of careless glee,
To whom the whole world seemed a dream
    Of song and revelry!
There came a change ere sunset:
    And the mirthful, heedless youth
Awoke, henceforth to look on life
As a holy battle-field of strife,
    Of earnestness and truth!

"I had seen the youthful Kaiser,[3]
    And gave admiring heed
To the housings, wrought in blue and gold,
    Of his Andalusian steed:
I had marked his lordly bearing,
    And owned the stern appeal

Of the Austrian lip, astute and firm,
  And proud eye of Castile.
I had seen his Flemish warriors,
  With plume and gilded spur;
And pampered Andalusian lords,
  In silk and miniver.
My eyes were dazed with gazing
  On corslet and on helm,
As they thronged the city's northern gate,
And passed in slow, imperial state,
  To the Diet of the realm.
But it was not prince nor pageant
  That wrought my spirit's change,
And Kaiser Karl was not the man
  To move a work so strange.

" The Herald of the empire,[4]
  Robed in official garb,

Had sped on high commission forth,
   Upon his milk-white barb.
He forded many a river,
   Crossed many a mountain-chain,
And threaded many a forest-path,
   And scoured o'er many a plain.
He passed by princely castles,
   And cities of renown,
But paused—before the lowly gate
   Of a grey old Saxon town!
The rude and rugged pavement
   Is ringing 'neath his feet,
As the milk-white barb is pacing slow
   Along the dusky street.
All knew that rider's mission,
   And why he came in state,
And drew his rein, and bent his plume
   Beneath the convent-gate:—
For a strong voice, from that portal,
   Had echoed far and near,

And had mutter'd 'mongst the seven hills,
  And made Rome quake for fear!—
Aye!—from a poor monk's cloister
  A tempest had been hurl'd,
Whose mighty heavings were to shake
  The prison of a world!

" ' Thy Kaiser, *Martin Luther!*
  And the Diet of the State,
Do cite thee thither to repair
  Within a certain date.
He covenants ' Safe-Conduct,'
  And, to assure thy weal,
He signs the mandate with his name,
  And seals it with his seal.'

" There was sighing in the cloister,
  There was wailing in the town:—
' Alas! our Brother goeth forth
  To win the martyr's crown!

We've heard of perjur'd councils —
 Of violated bond —
And of the plighted, broken troth
 Of Kaiser Sigismond!'5

" But, 'midst the reeds that trembled
 Before the gathering storm,
E'en like some deeply-rooted oak
 Stood Luther's dauntless form.
Exultant amidst peril,
 Forth goes he to fulfil —
In face of friend, in face of foe —
 God's and his Kaiser's will.6

" Oh the throbbings of men's bosoms,
 Oppress'd by doubt and fear ! —
Oh the surgings of the multitude,
 As that poor monk drew near !

From hamlet and from city
    Around his feet they press;—
Some came to curse the heretic,
    And some the saint to bless.
' Cursed be the bold arch-rebel!'
    Was mutter'd 'mongst the crowd;
' God bless the man whom Rome hath cursed!'
    Responded clear and loud.
And many a peasant-mother—
    At cot, or cabin-door—
Held up her little babe, to see
    The teacher of the Poor.

" I mind me how I mingled
    Amongst the eddying throng,
And how my youthful steps were borne
    With torrent force along.—
I mind me how the Herald
    Pranced, foremost in the band,

And the Empire's Eagle spread its wings
    Upon his gilded wand ;—
And next, my young eye singled,
    From out the troublous scene,
One steadfast brow, *one* fearless eye,
    One calm, heroic mien —
A rock, whose base the surges
    Swept round, but could not move—
Conversing with his soul within,
    And with his God above!

" With that one look, fast faded
    Life's pageantry away!—
Aye, Boy! the masquerade was o'er—
    I gazed no more that day!

"Uprose the dewy morning,
 And gemm'd the vines with pearl,
And waken'd to their matin-song
 The throstle and the merle —
Waken'd the troublous city
 To the battle-field of life,
And woke the monk of Wittenberg
 To the trumpet-call of strife.
Uprose the weary princes
 From brief, perturb'd repose :
And from his purple couch of state
 Young Kaiser Charles arose !

"Bring forth the golden flagons,
 And pour the red wine free ;
And fill your goblets to the brim,
 From casks of Burgundy !
And for the lists now nerve ye,
 At yon imperial board,

And in the lordly banquet-hall
    Be your dull strength restored!
For Rome's unconquer'd rebel
    Hath weapons well anneal'd;
And his girdle he is bracing *now*,
    And polishing his shield!

" He hath enter**è**d his closet,
    And, kneeling prostrate there,
He is pouring forth his troubled soul
    In sighs, and tears, and prayer![7]
God help thee, Martin Luther!
    Thy Lord hath hid His face,
And, for a season, seal**è**d up
    The treasury of grace.
Oh, how the strong man wrestled!—
    Oh, how the weak man cried!—
But he knows the Angel's " Secret Name,"
    And will not be denied.[8]

Amidst thick clouds of darkness,
　　He knows that name is Love,
And that the anchorage of faith
　　Nor earth nor hell can move!

" I mind me how I marvelled,
　　As I stood without, and heard
The pleadings of that broken heart,
　　And how my soul was stirr'd.
I knew not, then, the dealings
　　Of a Father with a Son;
Nor how, apart from carnal strength,
　　The victory is won.
If sever'd from the mighty,
　　How weak the strong!—how faint!—
And, parted from the Saviour,
　　How helpless is the Saint!

" But the footstep of the herald
  Is ringing on the stair!—
The hour hath struck, and at its call
  He rises up from prayer.9
Like ocean, whose wild tumult
  Is hush'd at summer even,
Now calmly on his settled brow
  Resteth the light of heaven.
Behold, once more, the Dauntless
  With firm step moves along!—
He feels the *Rock* beneath his feet,
  And therefore is he strong.

" I ween that earth ne'er witnessed
  So lordly an array
Of princes and of potentates
  As met in state that day—
From the banks of yellow Tyber,
  From Danube's moaning river,

From Weser, Elbe, and Vistula,
  And flowery Guadalquiver: [10]
There were stout Teutonic barons,
  And proud Castilian lords,
And Belgic and Burgundian knights,
  Clanking their jewell'd swords;
There was cloth of gold from Flanders,
  Pearls from the Indian main,
And silks from Asiatic looms,
  And a new world's gold from Spain.

"The Empire's seven Electors,[11]
  Each in his chair of state,
Next to their Kaiser's gilded throne,
  In proud precedence, sate.
I mark'd our youthful monarch,
  Beneath his purple dome,
As whisper'd in his listening ear
  The Legate priest from Rome.

I marked the cruel cunning
  That lit Duke Alva's eye,
And the cloud across the anxious brow
  Of noble Saxony.[12]

" ' Will he retract ?'— Behold him,
  Before ye dare respond !—
Is *that* a man to league with Truth,
  And then to break his bond ?—
To turn again to darkness —
  Back, from the light of day—
To find a pearl of priceless worth,
  And fling that pearl away?

" ' Wilt thou renounce thy doctrines ?'
  ' Yea !— should they not accord
With Truth unchangeable, declared
  In God's unerring Word.

The mind of man is erring,
    Though honest be its aim —
The mind of God infallibly,
    Immutably, *the same!*
Prove ye that Christ and Luther
    Two gospels do declare,
And Luther's voice shall be the first
    His tenets to forswear;
But, failing this, my conscience
    Will not, and dare not, yield
To any Standard but the Lord's,
    In any battle-field!
Try, by God's word, each doctrine
    I've taught by speech or pen.—
My Kaiser!—here I take my stand,
    God helping me!—Amen!" [13]

" There was silence in the council,
    And men with awe look'd pale,

And cruel Alva knit his brow,
  And the Legate priest did quail.
'Twas strange!—*Here* sate a monarch,
  'Neath whose imperial sway
(Own'd in two earthly hemispheres)
  Ne'er sets the light of day;
And *here*, earth's rich and noble—
  Helms, mitres, coronets—
Back'd by the golden bribes of Rome,
  And, failing these, her threats!
And *there*, before his judges,
  Upheld by voice of none,
Stood a poor monk from Wittenberg—
  A simple miner's son—
Leaning upon an anchor,
  Within the riven veil,
And clasping to his breast the Word
  That cannot change nor fail!

" Thus, like some Alpine summit,
    Calm in the light of heaven,
While, round its agitated base,
    Dark thunder-clouds are driven:
In peace, though 'sieged by tempests —
    'Midst tumult, yet at rest —
There stood the man whom Rome hath curst,
    But whom his Lord hath blest!

" Will he retract? — First turn ye
    The planets from their course,
Or dash the mighty cataract
    Back to its mountain-source!

" My tale is well-nigh ended —
    The Empire's heavy ban

Hath echoed back the thundering curse
  Hurl'd from the Vatican!
What boots man's wrath?—The banner
  Of Christ hath been unfurl'd,
And a poor Saxon monk becomes
  The Hero of a world!

" The Branded and the Outcast
  A refuge-tower hath found,
Where—Patmos-like—the pen is free,
  And the wing'd soul unbound:
And where the holy Volume,
  Seal'd up, from age to age,
(For only priests and letter'd men
  Could read its learned page)
Became the poor man's treasure,
  Unroll'd by Luther's hand,
And vocal with the living speech
  Of the German's Fatherland—

The speech in which the mother
    Doth with her child converse —
The speech in which the silver-hair'd
    Life's toils and cares rehearse.

" And thus Truth's lamp was lifted,
    By God's o'erruling will,
From shadows of a convent-cell
    And set upon a hill.
It hath lighten'd northern forests,
    It hath smiled in Alpine glens,
And the valleys of the Island Queen
    Have shouted glad '*Amens!*'

" The curse, the ban, the Wartburg,
    But veil'd God's glorious ways;
And the echo to the wrath of man
    Is heard in songs of praise ![14]

" Aye, Boy! — the mightiest weapon
   Is not thy steel-wrought sword :
The bravest warrior of his age
   Is the servant of the Lord!"

NOTES.

Note 1, page 50.

"Tell of the sealy dragon,
   'Neath Siegfred's mighty hand."

According to the *Niebelungenlied*, it was on the borders of the Rhine, nearly opposite the present city of Worms, that Siegfred, the favourite hero of song and story, destroyed the dragon.

Note 2, page 51.

"It was a spring-tide morning."

It was in spring, on the morning of the 16th of April, 1521, that Luther arrived at Worms, where the Diet had already been sitting more than three months.

Note 3, page 53.

"I had seen the youthful Kaiser."

The Emperor Charles V. was born at Ghent in 1500, and

was, therefore, twenty-one years of age at the period of this celebrated Diet. He was the eldest son of Philip, archduke of Austria, and of Joanna, the daughter of Ferdinand of Arragon and Isabella of Castile.

Note 4, page 54.

"The Herald of the empire."

Everlasting blessings to the soul of the imperial herald, Gaspar Sturm, were the consequences of this mission. His intercourse with Luther during the journey, and Luther's sermons at Weimar, at Eisenach, and at Erfurth, in all which places he was permitted to preach, wrought so powerfully on his convictions, that from henceforth Gaspar Sturm was a staunch friend of Luther and of the Reformation. When Luther left Worms to return to Saxony, the herald joined him again at Oppenheim, near Frankfurt, and accompanied him as far as Freundsberg. There they parted as dear brothers in Christ.

Note 5, page 57.

"We've heard of perjur'd councils —
Of violated bond —
And of the plighted, broken troth
Of Kaiser Sigismond!"

John Huss, the great Bohemian reformer, was executed at Constance, July 7th, 1415, notwithstanding a formal "safe-conduct" from the Emperor Sigismond.

Note 6, page 57.

"Exultant amidst peril,
Forth goes he to fulfil —
In face of friend, in face of foe —
God's and his Kaiser's will."

Luther's ready and determined obedience to the imperial summons, in the face alike of warning and of threat, unfolds a noble example of Christian intrepidity. Even the most stout-hearted of his friends implored him to take warning from the history of the past, and abide in a place of safety. But Luther knew that the hour was come for setting the candle upon the candlestick, that it might give light to the world; and his own life was only dear to him as an offering to Christ. "If," said he, "every tile on every house-roof at Worms were a devil, yet still I would go."

Many years afterwards, when the great reformer was drawing near to life's evening, he alluded to the emotions of exultant joy which he experienced at that hour, saying to his friends, "I felt no fear. God can give marvellous boldness. If the same thing had happened now, instead of then, I am not sure that I should feel such extraordinary liberty and exultation."

Note 7, page 61.

"He is pouring forth his troubled soul
In sighs, and tears, and prayer."

It was even said of Luther's Divine Master, "It pleased the Father to bruise Him." And so, in a different sense, and for a widely different end, it may be said of the servant. One of the most affecting historical documents in existence is that which records his mental agony under a temporary sense of Divine desertion, as the hour drew near for his introduction to the Diet. His friends, who were waiting for his reappearance, outside the door of his closet, heard his earnest, agonising pleadings with his God and Father. For awhile a horror of thick darkness seems to have veiled the Mercy-seat. "O God!" he pleaded; "O God! Oh, Thou, my God! help me against all the wisdom of this world. Do this, I beseech Thee! Thou *shouldst* do this; . . . . by Thine own mighty power! . . . . The work is not mine, but Thine. I have no business here. . . . . I have nothing to contend for with these great men of the world! I would gladly pass my days in happiness and peace. But the cause is Thine . . . and it is righteous and everlasting! O Lord, help me! O, faithful and unchangeable God! I lean not upon man. It were vain! Whatever is of man is tottering; whatever proceeds from him must fall! My God! my God! Dost not Thou hear? My God! Art Thou no longer living? Nay, Thou canst not die! Thou dost but hide Thyself. Thou hast chosen me for this work. I know it! . . . Therefore, O God, accomplish Thine own will! Forsake me not, for the sake of Thy well-beloved Son, Jesus Christ, my defence, my buckler, and my stronghold!"

Then, after a moment of silent struggle, Luther continued:—"O Lord! where art Thou? . . . My God! where art Thou? . . . Come, I pray Thee; I am ready! . . . Behold me prepared to lay down my life for Thy truth! . . . suffering like a lamb! For the cause is holy. It is Thine own! . . . I will not let Thee go!

No, nor yet for all eternity! And though the world should be thronged with devils, and though this body, which is the work of Thine hands, should be cast forth, trodden under foot, cut in pieces . . . consumed to ashes . . . MY SOUL IS THINE! Yes! I have Thine own Word to assure me of it. My soul belongs to Thee, and will abide with Thee for ever! Amen! O God, send help! . . . Amen!"

See D'Aubigné's *History of the Reformation*, Eng. trans., vol. ii. page 289. See also Michelet's *Life of Luther*.

Merle D'Aubigné says that this prayer may be originally found " dans le Recueil des Pièces relative à la comparation de Luther, à Worms, sous le numero 16; au milieu de 'Sauf-conduits,' et d'autres documents de ce genre."

NOTE 8, page 61.

" But he knows the Angel's 'Secret Name,'
And will not be denied."

Genesis, xxii. 26–29.

NOTE 9, page 63.

" The hour hath struck, and at its call
He rises up from prayer."

" Four o'clock arrived. The marshal of the empire appeared. Luther prepared to set out. God had heard his prayer: he was calm when he quitted the hotel."—D'AUBIGNÉ.

NOTE 10, page 64.

"From the banks of yellow Tyber,
From Danube's moaning river,
From Weser, Elbe, and Vistula,
And flowery Guadalquiver."

"And now the doors of the hall were thrown open. Luther entered; and many who constituted no part of the Diet gained admission with him. Never had any man appeared before so august an assembly."— D'AUBIGNÉ.

NOTE 11, page 64.

"The Empire's seven Electors."

Only six of the seven electors of the empire were present on this occasion.

NOTE 12, page 65.

"And the cloud across the anxious brow
Of noble Saxony."

Frederick, surnamed the Wise. Elector of Saxony, was Luther's dear friend. It is a remarkable fact that they never met, face to face, till this hour; and, it is believed, never afterwards, till they met in heaven. The Duke of Alva, afterwards so famous (or rather so *infamous*) in the history of Protestantism, and his two sons, were present.

Note 13, page 60.

"*My Kaiser!—here I take my stand,
God helping me!—Amen!*"

"Hier stehe Ich! Ich kan nicht anders.
Gott helfe mir! Amen!"

Note 14, page 70.

"And the echo to the wrath of man
Is heard in songs of praise."

"Surely the wrath of man shall praise thee; and the remainder of wrath shalt thou restrain."— Psalm lxxvi. 10.

LAY OF THE WARTBURG.

"Sint Scripturæ quæ deliciæ meæ! Nec decipior in eis, nec decipiam ex eis."— AUGUSTINE.

THERE was mourning on the banks of Elbe,
    In the laughing month of May;
In town and hamlet, hall and cot,
    Were sorrow and dismay.
There were boding sighs, and childlike tears,
    By strong men freely shed;
And broken words—" Let foes beware—
Kaiser or Pope—if they but dare
To crush one single, honour'd hair
    Upon that freeborn head!

" We care not for tiara crowns,
    Nor royal miniver !
The Saxon hath his coat of mail,
    And steed, and knightly spur !
We care not for the golden keys ;
    We have our iron fist ;
And thousand voices shall demand
The birthright of the Fatherland,
If Rome dare lay her crimson'd hand
    On Truth's evangelist."

There are haughty questionings and frowns,
    In proud, imperial hall ;
There was jubilee in Vatican,
    And on the Quirinal ;
And the ruddy wine-cup brimmeth o'er
    At many a festal board,
Because Rome dreams her stubborn foe
Hath pluck'd the arrow from his bow,
    And sheathed his daring sword.

There kneels an unknown captive Knight
    In a solitary tower;
And he rises up to trim his lamp
    At evening's shadowy hour.
The dark pine-forests wave beneath,
    With hollow, troublous sighs;
And the old oaks gather up the sound,
And send the moaning cadence round,
    And the ivied tower replies.

A soldier of a mighty King
    To Him his knee hath bow'd,
And the service of a duteous Knight
    Most loyally hath vow'd;—
'Twas He who gave the hand its sword,
    And gave the breast its shield;—
A King whose foemen he hath braved,
And glorious banner sternly waved
    In many a battle-field!

I ween men thought it strange to see
   Such stalwart cavalier,
(With hilted sword, and casque, and plume,
   And all a bold knight's gear),
With studious brow, so lined with thought,
   And introverted eye,
And hand endow'd with clerkly skill,
Guiding with energetic will
The movements of a vigorous quill,
   As hour by hour rolled by.

Now swept he royal David's harp
   With firm, yet reverent hand,
Making it vocal with the words
   Of his own Fatherland;[1]—
Now bade the Saxon's mother-tongue
   Proclaim, in household word,
The high and holy doctrines taught,
And glorious deeds of wonder wrought,
   By David's King and Lord.

The summer came, with gifts to earth —
    Sunshine and balmy shower —
Lengthening the ivy's muffling clasp
    Around the ancient tower;
And Autumn, with her ripening suns,
    Storm-clouds, and ruddy gleams,
And mellow fruits, and garnered sheaves,
And sobbing winds, and rustling leaves,
    And flashing mountain-streams.

"Rise up, Sir Knight! I ween thy brow,
    With hard soul-conflicts lined,
Will throb less hurriedly if fann'd
    By the cool forest-wind.
Come forth, and join the jovial troop
    Who rise, with morrow's dawn,
And leave the Wartburg's gloomy tower,
The breezy woodland-paths to scour,
    With hawk, and hound, and horn!"[2]

*　　　*　　　*　　　*

*　　　*　　　*

The jasper portals of the morn
  In silence backward roll'd,
And pour'd upon the waking earth
  A flood of molten gold.
The old oak doors in Wartburg tower
  Creak'd open, one by one;
The spurs are clattering in the yard,
The heavy fastenings are unbarr'd,
  And the gates are backward thrown.

There were noble knights and sturdy squires,
  With plumes and sheathèd swords;
There were jägers, with their winding horns,
  And jests and wrangling words.

The Landgraf, with his massive curb,
    Bridled his chafing steed;
And the spicy " stirrup-cup" went round,
And horse and rider, hawk and hound,
    The castle-gate have freed.

'Twas not to marshal feats of arms
    That the shrill clarion blew,
But for the peaceful forest-chase—
    The wild-wood *rendezvous!*
And many a noble stag who browsed,
    That morn, in antler'd pride,
Sobb'd out his life on upland fell,
Or stood at bay in forest dell,
Ere the loud bugle's winding swell
    Sounded at eventide.

What rider and what gallant steed
    Were foremost in the chase,

And which excell'd in strength or skill,
   'Twere tedious to retrace.
Down forest-glades—o'er upland steeps—
   They strove with will and might;
And the solemn wild-wood rang with glee,
As shouted, loud and merrily—
   All—save the Wartburg Knight!

They marvell'd what might be his crest,
   And what his pedigree;
And yet they read upon his brow
   Truth, Trust, and Loyalty!—
A hand unused to rein a steed,
   Or wear a jewell'd ring,
And yet an eye whose fire might grace
The loftiest line, the proudest race,
With a bold sparkle that might face
   Kaiser, or Pope, or King!

'Twas plain to see that soul like his
    Breathed not her native air,
Amid the death-wail and the shout,
    The tumult and the glare.
Leagued with the strong against the weak,
    He sighed, and stood apart.
Oh! he could well-nigh bare his breast,
Between oppressor and oppressed,
    And hug the bitter dart.

When the poor quarry wounded sank,
    And triumph-shouts rose high,
He only saw, of sin and grief,
    The symboled mystery.
And big tears, down his manly cheek,
    In heavy drops would roll:
"Alas!" he sighed; "behold the way
Sin's Antichrist doth still waylay,
And hunt his feeble, trembling prey,
    The deathless human soul!"

Anon, he spied a leveret
    Entangled in a snare;
And then he brake the subtle toils,
    And freed the trembling hare.
He wrapped her softly in his cloak,
    With strangely gentle hands;
" Thus would I snatch from sin's control,
Thus would I, in love's mantle roll
(Heaven grant me grace!) the fettered soul,
    And crush Rome's deadly bands!"

There were who list the strange Knight's words,
    And stopped, and looked aghast;
But others gave their steeds the spur,
    And bounded fleetly past:
And others sent a jovial laugh
    Adown the forest aisle;
But the Landgraf gave his plume a toss,
And with young Johann of the Schloss[3]
    Exchanged a conscious smile.

Yet neither Johann of the Schloss,
    Nor yet the Landgraf guessed,
What labouring thoughts are wrestling hard
    Within that true Knight's breast.
His soul is gathering up her strength,
    His Master's cross to bear;
In weakness — taking hold of might,
In darkness — stretching forth to light,
Watching for morning through the night,
    In the energy of prayer.
He is learning how his Lord can work
    Without his feeble aid;
How, for Christ's glory, man's renown
    Must choose the valley's shade.
He is hurried from the battle-field,
    And taught to sheathe *his* sword,
For one brief space — one restless span,
That the great work his voice began,
Be not achieved by might of man,
    But by the *Spirit's Word*.

Less need for Luther's rousing voice,
   By altar and by hearth,
Soon as the Gospel's silver trump
   Christ's message soundeth forth!
Less need that Luther's urn of clay
   Truth's precious drops should pour,
Soon as the living waters glide,
Freely and full in native tide,
   By cot and cabin door.

When, from the Wartburg's Patmos shades,
   Christ's own true Knight shall come,
With the Saxon's Bible in his hand,
   For the Saxon's hearth and home;
When God's own Gospel shall declare
   The strength of man as vain,
The Spirit's sword of heavenly might
Shall carve Truth's pathway through the fight,
And out of darkness bringing light,
   The Lord alone shall reign!

NOTES.

Note 1, page 82.

"Now swept he royal David's harp
With firm, yet reverent hand,
Making it vocal with the words
Of his own Fatherland," &c.

Luther's captivity in the Wartburg was an interval from personal action replete with the most important results to the dawning Reformation. "Before this time," writes Merle D'Aubigné, " Luther had translated some fragments of the Holy Scriptures. . . . These earlier essays had been eagerly bought up, and had awakened a general demand for more; and this desire on the part of the people was regarded by Luther as a call from God. He resolved to meet it. He was now a captive, enclosed within lofty walls; but what of that? He wanted this time of leisure to render the Word of God into the language of his nation. Soon shall we see that *Word* descending with him from the Wartburg, circulating among the families of Germany, and enriching them with spiritual treasure, hitherto shut up within the hearts of a few pious persons. . . . Thenceforth the Reformation was no longer in the hands of the Reformer. The BIBLE was brought forward, and Luther held a secondary place. The Reformer placed the BOOK in the hands of the people; thenceforth each might hear God Himself speaking to him: and as for Luther, he mingled in the crowd, placing himself among those who came to draw from the common fountain of light and life."— *English Translation*, vol. iii. p. 39.

NOTE 2, page 83.

" Rise up, Sir Knight," &c.

" The life of the Doctor of Wittenberg, in his assumed character of Knight, had indeed, at times, a something about it truly theological. One day there was a grand preparation for a hunting party, and Luther, whose health was suffering from unwonted bodily inaction, was invited to join the chase. " The snares were made ready, the fortress gates thrown open, the dogs let loose. The huntsmen were in high spirits; the dogs scoured the hills, driving the hares from the brushwood. But as the tumult swelled around him, *the Knight George* (Luther's disguised name), motionless in the midst of it, felt his soul fill with solemn thoughts. Looking around him, his heart heaved with sorrow. 'Is not this,' said he, ' the very picture of the Devil, setting his dogs, the bishops, those messengers of Antichrist, to hunt down poor souls?' A young leveret had been snared; and Luther, rejoicing to liberate it, wrapped it in his mantle, and deposited it in the midst of a thicket. But scarcely had he left the spot when the dogs scented it, and killed it. Drawn to the place by its cry,

Luther uttered an exclamation of grief:—'O Pope! and thou too, O Satan! it is thus that ye would compass the destruction of the souls that have been seemingly rescued from death!'"— D'AUBIGNÉ, vol. iii. p. 20.

NOTE 3, page 88.

"And with young Johann of the Schloss."

Johann von Berlepsch was Provost of the Wartburg during Luther's imprisonment there.

THE HERMIT OF LIVRY.

A PAGE FROM FRENCH HISTORY OF THE FIFTEENTH CENTURY.

PART I.

> "For the most loved are they
> Of whom Fame speaks not, with her clarion voice,
>   In regal halls. The shades o'erhang their way;
> The vale, with its deep fountains, is their choice.
>   . . . .   And gentle hearts rejoice
> Around their steps."   FELICIA HEMANS.

Within an ancient forest lone,
    Beside a tinkling well,
An Eremite, long years agone,
    Had scooped his little cell.

With fragrant shootings of the pine
    He strewed the rock-hewn floor;

And trained the briery eglantine
    On either side the door.

He wove his couch with ozier wands,
    And laid his bed with moss;
And at its foot, with pious hands,
    He hung his beechen cross.

And when his vesper psalm was sung,
    At balmy close of day,
Within its cresset chain he hung
    His little lamp of clay.

No worldling's footstep dare disturb
    His sweet and placid hours;
Conning, perchance, some healing herb,
    Or watering his flowers.

The huntsman, with a bugle blast,
    Recalled the eager hound,

Long ere the chestnut shades were passed
    Which girt that cell around.

But helpless things, and wan, and weak,
    And sorrowful, and poor,
Knew well which narrow path to seek,
    To reach the hermit's door.

The wounded hare would fearless come,
    And drink beside his well;
The squirrel coved his winter home
    Within his mossy cell.

And forest birds of shyest mood
    Would flutter in and out;
And share his scanty dole of food,
    Without a fear or doubt.

But though, for every mortal ill,
    He mixed the balmy cup,

When wounded spirits craved his skill,
With all his pity and goodwill,
  He could not bind them up.

He could not give to soul's afaint
  The manna of the word;
He loved the legendary saint,
  Yet hardly knew his Lord.

He conned his missal o'er and o'er,
  And rung its changes round;
But of the Gospel's holy lore
  He scarcely knew the sound.

But He who heals the blind and halt,
  And breaks the captive's thrall,
Will soon, with larger trusts, exalt
  The faithful in the small.

It was the balmy month of May;
    And from his mossy bed
The hermit rose at break of day,
Just as the mavis on the spray
    His matin hymn had said;

Just as a slanting sunbeam stole
    Adown the forest aisle,
And fretted branch, and hoary bole,
    Grew ruddy with its smile;

Just as the lily's silver bell
    By morn's first breeze was shaken;
Just as the wild doe at the well
    Her morning thirst had slaken.

And when his missal's sweetest lay
    Had glided off his lip,
The hermit girt his hodden grey,
    And took his staff and scrip.

He took his failing cruise of oil,
    And eke his wallet scant,
To sue for alms, with patient toil,
    A lowly mendicant.

He slowly trod, with sandaled feet,
    The forest's dappled floor,
Singing his "*Paternosters*" sweet,
    And "*Aves*,"—o'er and o'er.

God's earth beneath — God's sky above,
    Throbbed as with life and light;
And yet the wondrous name of Love
    He could not read aright.

And as his spirit pondered o'er
    The viewless and the seen,
And listened to that river's roar
    Which darkly flows between,

His poor heart shivered on its bank,
And heard the billows toss,
But saw no barque, no bridge, no plank,
To bear him safe across.

PART II.

The lily's silver bell had tolled
    The sunset's dewy hour,
And holy Vespertide had rolled
Its fulgent waves of molten gold
    Adown the forest bower;

Filling each amber cup and bell,—
    Gilding each bough and shaft,—
Turning to chrysolite the well
    At which the wild doe quaffed.

The little birds, with look askant,
    Expect their wonted store;
The squirrel, pert and petulant,
    Is chafing at the door.

He comes! Oh gentle Eremite,
    With staff, and cross, and scrip;
What means that smile of heavenly light
    Which trembles on thy lip?

Say, hast thou scanned, like one of yore,
    A shining heavenward road,
Up which the sinful and the poor
    May climb direct to God?

Down which angelic pinions move,
    Bearing good gifts to men,
And answering messages of love
    Return to heaven again?

Perchance thy hands, with eager haste,
    This day have grasped a dole,
Sweeter than honey to the taste,
Dearer than well-spring in the waste,
    To the poor fainting soul.

The staff and scrip aside are laid ;
    The little lamp is trimmed ;
The evening psalm is softly said ;
The " *Paternoster* " prayer is prayed,
    But not one " *Ave* " hymned.

And when, within his coved cell,
    The squirrel slept serene,
And the pale lamp-light softly fell
    Upon the quiet scene ;

It lit the placid brow of age,
    All reverently bent
Over the glorious Gospel page
    Of Christ's NEW TESTAMENT.

The "*Compline*" hour unheeded went ;
    The "*Nocturn*" watch is gone ;
And still that reverent brow is bent,
    And still that eye reads on ;

Beholding where the Saviour dwelt,
 Dwelling with Him, in thought;
Kneeling, in spirit, where He knelt,
 And listening when He taught;

Launching upon the midnight sea,
 By the storm-pinion swept;
Talking with Christ at Bethany,
 And weeping when He wept;

Rising with Mary when she heard
 That her dear Lord was come;
Hearkening the resurrection word
 Of victory o'er the tomb;

Slow following to the Judgment-hall,
 With bitter tears — yet sweet;
Tasting the wormwood and the gall,
 Kissing the wounded feet;

Searching the dark tomb for the Dead;
    Hailing the shining vision;
And heeding what the angel said,—
    " *He is not here — but risen!*"

Meeting at Galilee the Christ;
    Noting each gracious word;
And, with the dear Evangelist,
    Exclaiming, " 'Tis the Lord!"

Looking up steadfastly on high,
    The while his Lord ascends,
And grasping the peace-legacy
    Of Jesus to His " friends!"

And ere the cresset lamp burned dull,
    And ere night's shadows part,
The Sun of Righteousness rose full
    On his rejoicing heart.

Now hath he cordials for the faint
    They never found before;
Medicines for every woe and plaint,
    And riches for the poor.

For wounded hearts, and sick, and sad,
    He hath a healing balm;
And for the whole, and young, and glad,
    A sweet thanksgiving psalm.

The poor dumb creatures of the grove
    His bounty still partake;
He loved them with a better love,
    For his dear Saviour's sake.

But most he loved the sinner's soul,
    And yearned to publish round,
The saving grace which made *him* whole,
    The heaven his heart had found.

So, with the name of Christ, his Lord,
    Engraven on his lip,
Goes forth a preacher of the Word,
    With Bible, staff, and scrip;

Receiving from the cold and stern
    The bitter herbs of strife;
And giving back, in sweet return,
    The heavenly Bread of life.

PART III.

The choristers, with hurried glee,
    Have chaunted the last psalm,
And the great bell swingeth heavily
    In the tower of Notre Dame!

And a city's life-blood, at the sound,
    Stops with a sudden start;
And then with strong convulsive bound,
Flows to one common central ground,
    As to its throbbing heart.

Through a hundred alleys, dark and deep,
    The black tide rushes on,
With roar, and swirl, and maddened leap,
    At the great bell's heavy tone.

The cripple seizes on his crutch,
    And staggers through the throng;
The squalid Mother in her clutch,
    Drags the scared child along.

The courtier clasps his baldrick bright
    O'er robe of miniver;
The hero from his hundredth fight
    Puts on his gilded spur.

The mitred Bishop mounts his mule,
    In rich caparison;
The theologian quits his school,
    In the halls of the Sorbonne.

The bridegroom leaves the feast and song;
    The monk his "Ave" psalm;
All—all to swell that surging throng,
    In the square of Notre Dame;

Where the ancient dial points the hour,
 As with the wand of death :
And the great bell swingeth in the tower,
 And the people yell beneath ;

All gazing, with the demon smile
 Of fratricidal Cain,
Upon a gloomy funeral pile,
 A stake, a torch, a chain !

And on the left, and on the right,
 A thousand tongues exclaim,
" Bring forth the impious Eremite,
 To death, and woe, and shame !"

And now a grim procession steers
 Its snake-like course along ;
With monks, and priests, and halberdiers,
Carving a pathway with their spears,
 Amidst the panting throng.

Who *is* he : with that soft, mild eye,
    So dulled by prison thrall ;
And that firm step of courage high,
And look of patient constancy,
    No terrors can appal ?

Who is he ? Ask the poor and low ;
    And ask the wan and sick ;
And ask the helpless if *they* know
    The impious heretic.

And ask the small birds of the air
    Who shared his scanty dole ;
And ask the lithe and frisking hare
    His gentle hands made whole.

And ask the sinful of his skill,
    And let the saved repeat,
How beautiful upon the hill,
    Were once those fettered feet !

But the great bell swayeth to and fro,
    In the tower of Notre Dame;
And heavily, and harsh, and slow,
    They chaunt the funeral psalm.

He heareth not the dolorous hymn,
    Nor heeds the rush and roar;
He is walking by a river's brim,
And listening to the Seraphim
    Upon the farther shore.

He is standing by a river's bank,
    But sees no billows toss;
And asks no barque, no bridge, no plank,
    To bear him safe across.

For he sees a chariot as of fire,
    With wheels of scorching flame;
And then the angel-song grew nigher,
    And Jesus quickly came.

Thus rose he to the realms of bliss,
　Glorious — yet silently ;
And left no name on earth but this —
　" THE HERMIT OF LIVRY."

Yet in the courts of light and love
　His name is brightly graven ;
His praise is registered above,
　His record is in heaven.

SCRIPTURE LYRICS.

THE BOY OF LYSTRA.

PART I.

"And that from a child thou hast known the Holy
Scriptures."—2 *Tim.* iii. 15.

The morning breeze was sighing
   O'er Lystra's arid plain;
And slowly waved the dark stone pine,
And fanned the clusters of the vine,
   And stirred the rustling grain.
An orient streak was paling
   The rising matin star;
They said it was the golden fringe
   Of bright Apollo's car!

And there be warbling voices,
   In dreamy fall and swell,

From maidens, bearing empty urns
   Adown the olive dell;
And singing, as they pass along,
The snatches of a choral song
   To the Naiad of the well.

And from the city portal
   Rolls forth a pæan sound,
From white-robed priests with flowing hair
   In golden fillets bound;
Chaunting the mighty triumphs
   Of Lystra's sceptred Jove;
While to his colonnaded fane,
Timing their footsteps to the strain,
   In stately file they move.

But hush! Whence steals that warbling,
   So soft and liquid clear?
Sure, never muse from Phocian Mount,
Nor nymph from Ida's sweetest fount,
   Hath tuned that dulcimer!

Three voices!—*one*,—though chastened
   By time, still led the hymn :
But *one* might e'en have caught its tone
   From far-off Seraphim !
And *one*,—the ringing treble,
   As of some sweet-voiced boy,
Whose heart was full of echo-haunts
   For notes of love and joy !

Their speech is of a country
   Beyond the purple hills ;
Nor wafted by Thessalian breeze,
Nor taught by fair Pierides,
   Beside Castalian rills.
They sang like Amram's daughter
   Beside dark Egypt's sea :
They sang as royal David sung,
The while his cunning hand he flung
   O'er harp and psaltery.

Though the Boy's accent hinted
  Of Hellas' classic prime,
And of a Grecian Father's tongue,
  And fair Ægean clime.

'Twas beautiful,—beholding
  Those Hebrew mothers sweet,
And that high-browed and earnest youth,
Who listened to the words of truth,
  Reclining at their feet;
Spell-fastened by a Volume,
  Unrolled upon his knee;
— The pæan chorus rose on high,
Nor flushed his cheek, nor fired his eye,
And maidens, from the well, went by,
  Nor stirred his reverie.

What unseen treasure hideth
  Within that ancient scroll?

No graceful lore seems lettered there,
In fair Hellenic character,
   To trance his heaven-born soul.
His thoughts are in that country,
   Beyond the purple hills:
A land of showers and fruitful vales,
Of balmy dews and spicy gales,
   Of fountains and of rills.
With kindling eye he questions
   The dim and faded scroll:
Striving to weave, midst many a sigh,
The golden threads of prophecy,
With holy type and promise high,
   In one harmonious whole.

He reads of sceptred Judah:
   Of Jessie's royal stem:
He readeth of a Branch of might,
A Star to rise on Israel's night,
A throne of everlasting light,
   A glorious Diadem!

When prostrate kings shall worship,
　　And subject tribes shall fear;
And Gentile nations shall behold,
And bring their incense and their gold,
　　And far-off sons draw near;
The waste shall bud like Eden,
　　And desert places bloom:
Then spake the Boy, with glistening eyes,
" Oh *when* shall Judah's Sceptre rise?
When dawn the Star on Israel's skies?
　　When shall the kingdom come?

" So long! so long, my Mother!
　　Why tarrieth He so late?"
" My son, the while He seems to stay,
He girdeth on His bright array;
His chariot wheels are on the way:—
　　Blessed are they who wait!"

PART II.

"The gods are come down to us in the likeness of men."—
Acts. xiv. 2.

Thrice blest were they who waited
   The day-spring from on high;
Blest were they, through the shades of night,
Blest at the dawning of the light,
And blessed with blessings kept in sight
   By Faith's unwearied eye.

According as it listeth
   So blows the wind of heaven;
According to appointed hour,
As drops the dew on upturned flower,
   So was the blessing given.

Yet many a breeze of morning
    Still sighed o'er Lystra's plain,
And murmured in the dark stone pines,
And shook the ripe fruits from the vines,
    And swept the golden grain.
Still, at the city portal,
    The crippled beggar lay;
And still in purple robe, swept by
The rich man with averted eye,
    Exultant on his way.
And still, at dewy morning,
    And still at evening's calm,
Awoke the same sweet symphony
From dulcet harp, and psaltery,
And woke those Hebrew voices three,
    Chaunting the holy psalm.

But look! Whence come those Strangers
    Who stand at Lystra's gate?

The one, with calm, benignant face,
With lofty brow and winning grace,
Moves forward with a stately pace,
   As of no mean estate.
And one, of meaner stature,
   Treads firm in hidden might.
Sure, none could ever search that eye
Of strong concentered energy,
   And e'er forget its light.
That brow — how firm! how earnest!
   That look — how keen, yet mild!
That changing cheek, whose rapid glow
Speaks of quick feelings, free to flow
Forth to all human hearts below,
   Down to each lisping child!
A heart whose boundless yearnings
   Encompass land and sea.
Poor cripple! will he pass *thee* by?
Think'st thou he notes thy whispered sigh?
Perchance if thou, in faith, draw nigh,
   He hath an alms for thee.

There rung a wild, strange chorus
    That hour, through Lystra's street.
Torches were tossing in the air,
Flamens rushed by with frenzied glare,
And women, with unbraided hair,
    Loose zones, and tinkling feet.
With triumph-shout and pæan
    The stifling air was rent:
" The gods revisit earth again :
Hail, Jove ! great king of gods and men !
    Hail, Hermes, eloquent !
Hail to the son of Chronos !
    Hail to the Pleiad-born !
The gods descend with healing art,
The lame man leapeth as a hart,
Woes of the iron age depart ;—
    Hail to earth's golden morn !
Garland the milk-white heifer !
    Bring rams with curving horn !
Hail to old Saturn's mighty son,
The thunderer of the ivory throne !
    Hail to the Pleiad-born !"

The glittering axe is lifted,
   The milk-white victim stands,
Fondling the hand prepared to slay,
And in her mild, unconscious play,
   Cropping her flowery bands.

The flashing steel, uplifted,
   Is shimmering in the light:
"*Hold!*" speaks a voice, at whose command
The axe reels in the flamen's hand,
And men in mute inquiry stand,
   Controlled by viewless might.
" We be not gods, but mortals ;
   With passions like your own.
We come to turn your lightened eyes
From idol rite and sacrifice,
   To serve one God alone.
One living God! Oh, Lystrians!
   The Heaven of heavens is His:
He framed it by His own decree,
He made the earth, the sky, the sea.

And all that therein is.
Each season is his witness,
　That all He doth is good:
He gives the sunshine and the rain,
The fruitful field, the laughing plain,
　The gladness and the food!"

Oh, there were high debatings,
　That eve, in Lystra's street.
" Strange!—that with passions like our own,
Men scorn the thyrsis and the crown,
And glory, homage, all cast down,
　As at a master's feet!
An unseen Lord and Master:
　Beneath whose wondrous sway
Olympian gods stand disarrayed,
Discrowned, dethroned,—a myth, a shade;
And poets' tuneful dreamings fade,
　Like morning mists, away!"

PART III.

"And that, from a child, thou hast known the Holy Scriptures, which are able to make thee wise unto salvation; through faith which is in Christ Jesus."—2 *Tim.* iii. 15.

REST for the weary footstep!
  Sleep for the troubled eye!
Dews for faint flower and drooping bough!
Soft smoothings for the furrowed brow!—
Oh night, how angel-like art thou!
  How blest thy lullaby!
The drowsy breeze of summer
  Scarce sighs its interlude.
So hushed is every viewless string,
You almost hear the turtle's wing
  Stir o'er her nestled brood;

And the sweet Naiad of the spring,
In tinkling whispers answering
   The Dryad of the wood.

Calm o'er the slumbering city
   The steady planets roll;
And Pleiads their sweet influence pour,
As if a pitying love they bore
   For man's bewildered soul.

What means that light forthshining
   So steadily, yet pale,
Down from one casement's latticed height?
Too earthward for a planet's light,
And yet too pure, too mild, too slight,
   For earthly festival!

Amidst that dreaming city,
   None heed its feeble spark;

But angel watchers know the place,
And, poised on viewless wings, they trace
The shinings of the lamp of grace
   Within this household ark.

What see they here to rivet
   Such fixed, ecstatic gaze?
A single lamp, of flickering strength,
A scroll, in all its breadth and length,
   Unroll'd beneath its rays.
A great Apostle's finger
   Is moving o'er that scroll;
And letters dim shine forth like gold,
And shades obscure are backward roll'd,
And dark enigmas straight unfold
   Before his list'ners' soul.

'Twas beautiful to witness
   Those Hebrew mothers twain,

With folded hands and heavenward eye,
Clasping the message from on high,
Like autumn flowers, athirst and dry,
   Drinking the latter rain.

And thou, oh, young disciple!
   The child of faith and prayer;
What is it sweeps thy radiant brow
With something like the cypress bough,
As if a trailing cloud, e'en now,
   Had cast its shadow there?
Why doth thy yearning spirit
   Still wander down the scroll?
Still turning back to "Jesse's Stem,"
And sceptred Judah's diadem,
   Like needle to the pole?

Ah! there be low, soft breathings,
   Thy touch not yet hath stirred,

In the grand harp of prophecy;
And thy young hand hath passed these by,
   Unheeded and unheard.
Now bend thine ear to listen:
   And faith shall plume her wing,
And love, in holy reverence stand,
The while the great Apostle's hand
   Shall wake the plaintive string.

Behold, thine own Messiah,
   To work redemption's plan,
Must lay the regal vesture by,
And come "in great humility"—
   "*Emmanuel—God with man!*"
Behold the "Man of sorrows!"
   The lowly Virgin-born!
"Despised," "rejected," counted base,
And hiding not His smitten face
   "From spitting and from scorn!"

Behold the " bruised"—the " wounded!"—
 " The wormwood and the gall!"—
Behold the " Lamb to slaughter led,"
The victim, on whose dying head
 Were laid the sins of all!
" Accounted with transgressors ;"
 " Afflicted"—scorn'd—" abhorred!"—
Then spake the youth, with reverent brow,
" Messiah!—Christ!—I know Thee now!—
 Jesus!—my God!—my Lord!
I know Thee in Thy sorrow—
 Thine agony—Thy grief!
Love's wondrous heights I strain to span:
Oh, Son of God!—Oh, Son of Man!—
 Help Thou mine unbelief!

" Death could not break Thy sceptre :
 Thy kingdom *yet* shall come ;

And Gentile nations shall bow down,
And Israel's contrite sons shall own
Their Saviour's cross — their Ruler's crown —
 And come, with singing, home!"

THE BROTHERS.

"By faith, Abel offered unto God a more excellent sacrifice than Cain; by which he obtained witness that he was righteous; God testifying of his gifts: and by it he, being dead, yet speaketh."—*Heb.* xi. 4.

Though the opal gates of Eden
    Be for ever shut and barr'd;
Though to heaven, on mournful pinion,
    Back return'd the Angel-guard;

There was beauty in earth's ruins,
    Fragrance in her tangled bowers;
There was glory in the storm-cloud,
    And a star for midnight hours.

There was gladness in the sadness
  Of poor Eve, the while she smiled—
Smiled and wept, and sighed and ponder'd,
  O'er her first and new-born child:

Musing o'er her gotten treasure;
  Striving, in her infant's face,
To decipher holy meanings—
  Hidden blessings—germs of grace!

" Have I gotten from Jehovah
  The true, promised Seed?" she said;
" Sorely bruised my heel the serpent,
  But my Seed shall bruise his head."

Sometimes heavenward—sometimes childward—
  Her sweet, pensive brow she turn'd—
Broken melodies soft chanting,
  Which in Edenland she learn'd!

Soon to sadness turn'd all gladness,
  As the seasons swiftly flew,
And the firstling of her cradle
  On to wilful boyhood grew.

One by one, bright hopes have wither'd—
  One by one, dark fears unfold :
Sin hath canker'd Eve's young rosebud—
  Sin hath changed to dross her gold!

Proud and restless was his bearing,
  Passionate his eye, and wild ;
Strong in will, perverse, and froward—
  Such was Adam's first-born child.

Who shall say what boding anguish
  Planted in Eve's breast the thorn,
When she wove the osier cradle
  For her little second-born ?

Who shall say what early breathings
    Of the dove-like Spirit stole,
In the freshness of life's morning,
    O'er young Abel's quicken'd soul?

Child of Adam, earth-born, carnal,
    Offspring of a sinful race;
Son of wrath—yet heir of glory,
    Born of God—a child of grace!

Now, perchance, he loved to commune
    With his Mother, hand in hand,
Listening to her holy stories
    Of the vanish'd Edenland;—

Of the flowers that never wither'd,
    Of the fruits that ne'er decay'd,
Of the glory of the mountain,
    And the music of the glade;—

Of the holy angel-voices,
    Of the harpings heard from heaven,
Of sweet converse with Jehovah,
    In the cool and hush of even;—

Of the hour of sin and darkness,
    Of the Cherub's flaming sword,
Of God's plighted grace, in promise—
    Paradise by Christ restored!

Now, perchance, his flock he folded
    On the soft and dewy mead,
Pondering o'er his father's teachings,
    Why the spotless lamb must bleed;—

Why, upon Jehovah's altar,
    Blood of victim must be spilt,
Ere the rebel can be pardon'd,
    Ere the sinful wash'd from guilt!

Faith embraced the truth mysterious,
    Which the sign but dimly show'd;
Looking onward, as it ponder'd,
    To the Holy Lamb of God.

Years have flown,—nor fail'd to ripen
    Fruits of life and seeds of death:—
Cain's hard heart grew harder, darker—
    Abel's grew " from faith to faith."

Elder Brother! wherefore flasheth
    Proud defiance in thine eyes,
As the holy hour approacheth
    For the evening sacrifice?

On the upland stand two altars,
    In the balmy sunset air;
And the wood is set in order,
    And the Brothers twain stand there.

Abel owns himself a sinner,
    Needing the atoning blood ;
So he brings a spotless lambkin,
    At the bidding of his God.

Cain stood up, erect and haughty,
    And upon his altar heaped
Fruits of earth (a vain oblation !)
    His own hands had sown and reaped !

Can such offering, self-provided,
    Favour and acceptance find
With a holy God, who searcheth
    All the workings of man's mind ?

Cold upon the pile, unheeded,
    Cain's rejected offering lies ;
While a flood of heavenly glory
    Kindles Abel's sacrifice.

Upward, heavenward, thence ascending
    To the fount from whence it came,
Through the calm and perfumed ether,
    Rose the pure and holy flame.

Ah! what passions, fell and furious,
    Rush on Cain, in whelming flood,
Darken o'er his brow of hatred,
    And imbrue his hands in blood!

Turn we from the deed of darkness —
    Turn we from the crimson'd sod;
Heavenward turn we, where the spirit
    Of the " righteous" mounts to God!

Where the gates of pearl flew open,
    And Archangels veiled their face,
As they list the " *new song*," chaunted
    By the first of mortal race.

And the Seraphs paused to hearken
    To the music of that Name,
By a ransom'd soul first utter'd:—
    " *Worthy — worthy is* THE LAMB!

" 'Twas His grace that brought me hither—
    'Twas His hand my victory won:
No man cometh to the Father,
    But through merit of the Son.

" 'Twas the virtue of His life-blood *
    Wash'd my guilty soul from sin:
'Twas the mention of His merits
    Oped these gates, and let me in.

" 'Twas His Holy Spirit clothed me
    In this glorious robe of light;

---

* "The Lamb slain from the foundation of the world."— *Rev.* xiii. 8.

'Tis His Righteousness approves me
    Righteous in the Father's sight!"

*   *   *   *   *   *   *

Who is this? — the scathed and branded,
    Scorning to repent and live;
Seeking rest — yet finding torment; —
    Harden'd, guilty, fugitive!

All who saw him shunn'd the slayer;
    On his hand they knew the stain; —
Mothers whisper'd to their children,
    In a warning voice — " *'Tis his!*"

"WARNED OF GOD."

Hebrews, xi. 7.

Fair rolled the rivers in rejoicing flow;
   Bright fell the sunlight down on flowery glades;
And summer winds, in pulses soft and low,
   Breathed trembling music 'mid the quivering shades.

The purple mountains 'gainst a cloudless sky,
   Undimmed by portent of foreshadowing mist,
Bore up, in strength, the vaulted canopy,
   Like moveless pillars of bright amethyst.

Earth sat at ease! Her children up and down
   Paced restlessly; or idly dreamed among
Her festal bowers; or wove the nuptial crown;
   Or led the mazy dance, with harp and song.

And man was beautiful! His brow still told
    Of primal glory, fading fast away;
The noble image of its Godlike mould
    Still lingered round the tenement of clay.

The giant stature, and the stately grace;
    The lofty mien, unbent by toil or time;
The glowing beauty of the upturned face.
    Still bore the impress of a type sublime.

Earth sat at ease! Sin's lethal bowl was crowned
    With poison flowers; and men drank deep and laughed,
And passed the cup, from hand to hand, around;
    And counted bitter sweet, the while they quaffed.

They heard not (for their ears were waxèd dull)
    The wailing dirge the morning stars then sang,
'Stead of creation's birthsong beautiful,
    With which the vaulted dome of heaven erst rang.

They see not (for their eyes are waxen dim)
    That the full measure of their sins runs o'er ;
The cup of wrath is foaming to its brim
    Which Justice stands, with outstretched hand, to pour.

But hark ! Amid the dim old woods is heard
    The clang of axe. Then reeled the ancient oak ;
And the wild echoes of the hills are stirred
    With the sharp clangour of the hammer's stroke.

The mighty cedar shook his crashing boughs,
    And slowly bent to earth his lordly head ;
The lofty pines inclined their dusky brows,
    And balmy firs their resin tear-drops shed.

The ear of faith the gathering storm had heard ;
    The eye of faith had seen the uplifted rod ;
The work of faith was to obey God's word ;
    The hidden life of faith,—to "*walk with God.*"

Strong in their bands of sin, earth's son's deride
    The warning voice: and ask, with scornful lip,
" Where be the fountains of the whelming tide?
    Where rolls the sea to float thy mighty ship?"

But ever in the silence of the morn,
    And ever in the dewy hush of even,
The fragrant breath of sacrifice was borne
    Right upward to the glorious gates of heaven,

From one lone altar. Singly and alone,
    It witnessed to a world's apostate shame.
The Lord of grace vouchsafes that spot to own
    Where two or three are gathered in His name.

Men little knew how long the rod was stayed,
    By the uplifted hands of mighty prayer;
How long the hour of Justice was delayed,
    By virtue of the Love which pleaded there.

But man repented not; and pitying Love
    Would lose all glory if she dare depress
The sceptre of God's justice; or to move
    One pillar from His throne of righteousness.

Flee to the mountains — Death shall track thy flight!
    Hide in the valleys — Death arrives before!
Climb the wild peaks — cling to their craggy height:
    Death brooks no chain, no boundary, no shore!

Scale the tall tower — it crumbles into dust!
    Crouch with the trembling lion in his lair;
Hie to the forest — 'tis a worthless trust!
    Nest with the eagle — Death shall find thee there!

Launch the frail skiff — a crushed and shattered barque!
    Bind the firm raft — the black wave sucks it in!
Sinner! Salvation owns but one true Ark: —
    One Saviour conquers Death by conquering Sin!

AN ARK SONG.

Oh how buoyantly she rideth
    O'er the heaving billows dark!
Oh how safe is he who hideth
    In Salvation's only Ark!

Though the sun and moon be shaded,
    Quenched be every planet's spark,
Every orb of light be faded,
    There is light within the Ark!

Though without be fear and quailing,
    Cries of wild despair: yet hark!
'Midst the tempest's moan and wailing,
    Holy anthems glad the Ark!

Though no hand her helm be guiding,
    Though her course no compass mark,
Yet our Ship is safely riding,
    Love is pilot of the Ark!

Though man's hopes have perished wholly,
    Wrecked be every faithless barque,
For the trustful and the lowly
    There is room within the Ark!

Saviour! ere the floods assailed us,
    Ere each earthly lamp grew dark,
Ere the oil of gladness failed us,
    We repaired to Thee,—our Ark!

A VOYAGE FROM TROAS TO NEAPOLIS.

A.D. 53.*

"Come over into Macedonia and help us."—*Acts*, xvi. 9.

"Now weigh the anchor, mariners!
    And loose the flapping sail;
And turn our galley's curving prow
    Before the freshening gale.
O'er Ida's peak the paling stars
    Are fading, one by one;
And the Hours are harnessing the steeds
    Of bright Latona's son.
The sparkle of his chariot wheels
    Is glinting o'er the mountains;

* The first introduction of the Gospel into Europe.

And leaping down, with argent sheen,
  Are Ida's many fountains.
And many a Naiad, fast asleep,
  He wakens with a kiss;
And gilds Scamander's torpid stream,
  And ancient Simoïs.
And as he shakes his golden rein
  The flying axle glows,
And throws a smile across the isle
  Of classic Tenedos.
While, like a tide of chrysolite,
  From forth some orient font,
'Twixt glittering shores, down, downward pours
  The golden Hellespont!
And as he waves his fulgent locks
  O'er Lemnos, grey and cold,
Its shining coasts burst forth in light,
  As through a mist of gold.
On! on! and Ceres binds her sheaves,
  Midst Imbros' laughing bowers;[1]

And 'sacred Samothrace' looks o'er [2]
The purple line of bending shore,
As when old Homer sang of yore,
    Of Troy's beleaguered towers.[3]

"*Io Apollo!* On our helm
    Thy gold-tipt arrows shine;
And the swelling sail hath caught the breeze,
And our idle rowers, at their ease,
    Along their bench recline.
Steer for the Hespern!—to the land
    Of the Pythian's mystic shrine;
The laurel mount, and crystal fount,
    Dear to the tuneful Nine.
The land where a stainless robe of snow
    O'er Athos' shoulder falls:
The land of the Thunderer's ivory throne
    In bright Olympian halls!"

And so they steered;—and so they clave
    The blue Ægean sea;
And the chorus of the mariners
    Was shouted merrily;
And the listening dolphins heard the song,
    And tossed the foam-bells round,
And played around the shallop's wake
    As if they loved the sound;
And red libations were poured forth
    To fair Latona's son;
And the helmsman turned the vessel's prow
    Right on for MACEDON.

Ha! who be they? those Strangers four,[4]
    Who joined not in the song?
Who, when the foamy wine-cup poured
    Libations to the Pythian lord,
Sighed deep—and left the throng?
    Sighed—as in pity and in love,

And moved the lip in prayer,
Heavenward! as if up paths of light
They communed with some God of might,
Enthroned in glory there?

The seamen marvelled as they gazed
Upon these wondrous men;
And marvelled at the strange, new name,
(Unknown, unheard, till then),
Which dwelt, like music, on their lips,
Or like some fragrant balm,
Transmuting sorrow into joy,
And trouble into calm.
Such calm! They could not search its heights,
Nor sound those depths of joy,
Which nought on earth could give, or take,
Or 'minish, or alloy.

Well might they marvel, as they scanned
That Hebrew stranger's* mien;

* St. Paul.

His eye of consecrated fire,
   So steadfast and serene!
The moulding of that spacious brow,
   Where Reason held firm seat,
Sublimed by Faith, was never wrought
   At proud Gamaliel's feet:
Nay!—nor in Attic portico,
   Nor academic grove;
What subtle hand hath touched those lines
   Of tenderness and love?

Steer for the Hespern! He hath heard,
   Across the blue sea's foam,
A voice whose pleadings, strong and clear,
Are ringing in his thrilling ear,
   "*Come over!—help us!—come!*" 5
From continent, and creek, and isle,
   From mount, and forest shade,
Resound the echoes of that cry,
   "Come over to our aid!"

'Twas like the pleading of the sick
    For one to make him whole ;
'Twas like the agonising wail
    Of some poor, dying soul !—
'Twas like the cry of trav'ller, lost
    On some dark mountain side,
Groping around a precipice,
    And shouting for a guide !—
'Twas like some captive's hollow groan,
    Lifting his fettered hands,
And calling, in his wild despair,
    For one to break his bands !—
'Twas like the sob of those who weep,
    And find no comforter !—
On, for the West,—the throbbing West !
    God hath a people there!
There,—in the city's crowded mart ;
    There,—in the forest lone ;
There,—in the palaces of kings,
    Christ shall a people own.

There,—in the craggy Alpine heights,
    Echoing the eagle's cry,
The Lord will choose His witnesses
    To live for Christ,—or die.

There,—by the Moldau and the Elbe,
    By field, and fell, and flood,
The martyrs' fiery car will leave
    Its glorious track in blood.

There,—in a northern Isle afar,—
    A land of brooks and rills,
Of fountains and of depths, that spring
    From valleys and from hills;
A land whose sons are brave and free,
    Whose daughters, true and fair;—
God's gracious purpose marks that Isle;
    He hath much people there!

Away! Away! Again that cry;
    Again that sobbing moan;
" Come over!—over to our help!
    Come over to Macedon!"

Where Hæmus, girt with laurel zone,
    Lifts high his forehead bare;
On for Philippi's mural towers:
    God hath a people *there!*
A man of stern and iron will,
    Welded 'mid sin and strife;
Start not!—that gaoler's name is writ
    Within the book of life!
A woman, reaching forth her hands,
    Some viewless prize to win;
In lowly faith, content to wait,
Meekly, at Truth's strong outer gate,
    Till Love should let her in!

On! On!—The western hills grow red
    With the Day-god's parting kiss;
And the shallop tosses high the spray,
As she drops her anchor in the bay
    Of old Neapolis!

NOTES.

Note 1, page 154.

" . . Ceres binds her sheaves
Midst Imbros' laughing bowers."

Imbros was held sacred to Ceres.

Note 2, page 155.

" And 'sacred Samothrace' looks o'er
The purple line of bending shore."

"Sacred Samothrace."— Samothracia was the "*Monte Santo*" of the ancient Greeks. It was the cradle of many heathen rites and superstitions; and was, moreover, a safe and inviolable asylum for criminals and fugitives.

Note 3, page 155.

" As when old Homer sang of yore
Of Troy's beleaguered towers."

The author of *Eōthen* was much struck by the appearance of Samothrace, seen aloft over Imbros. He recollected how Jupiter is described in the *Iliad* as watching from thence the scene of the action before Troy. "Now I know," he says, "that Homer had passed along here; that this vision of Samothrace overtowering the nearer island was common to him and to me."

See Conybeare and Howson: *Life and Writings of Saint Paul*, vol. i. page 303.

Note 4, page 156.

. . . "those Strangers four."

The three companions of *Saint Paul*, in bearing the Gospel into Europe, were *Silas*, the sharer of his stripes and imprisonment, and the companion of the prison song; *Timothy*, his "own son in the faith," his "dearly beloved;" and *Luke*, "the beloved physician," the beautiful historian of the inspired narrative.

Note 5, page 158.

"Come over! — help us! — come!"

"And a vision appeared to Paul in the night; There stood a man of Macedonia, and prayed him, saying, Come over into Macedonia, and help us.

"And after he had seen the vision, immediately we endeavoured to go into Macedonia, assuredly gathering that the Lord had called us for to preach the Gospel unto them.

"Therefore loosing from Troas, we came with a straight course to Samothracia; and the next day to Neapolis;

"And from thence to Philippi . . ."—*Acts*, xvi. 9-12.

A SABBATH MORN AT PHILIPPI.

A.D. 53.

"Therefore loosing from Troas, we came with a straight course to Samothracia, and the next day to Neapolis;

"And from thence to Philippi, which is the chief city of that part of Macedonia, and a colony: and we were in that city abiding certain days.

"And on the sabbath we went out of the city by a river side, where prayer was wont to be made; and we sat down, and spake unto the women which resorted thither.

"And a certain woman named Lydia, a seller of purple, of the city of Thyatira, which worshipped God, heard us: whose heart the Lord opened, that she attended unto the things which were spoken of Paul."— *Acts*, xvi. 11-14.

    A FROWN on old Olympus!
    A smile on sunny vale!
A thousand thousand dewdrop globes
Upon the lily's bridal robes,
    And on the cistus pale!

Forth from the glowing Eastern
A flood of glory rolled;
Across the valley's flowery breast,
Across the Thracian mountains' crest,
Right forward to the throbbing West,
In waves like molten gold.

The snow-white mists of morning
Curled heavenward as they spread;
As if all earth, and sea, and sky
Put on their sabbath drapery;
All,—save one cloud, opaque and high,
Round old Olympus' head.

Why bend the reeds, low trembling,
Beside the river's lip?
Is it the footsteps, to and fro,
Of maidens, as they come and go,
With water-urns, down stooping low,
The limpid wave to dip?

Nay!— for the water lotos
Is anchored still at rest,
And not a ripple filleth up
Her steady alabaster cup,
   Borne on the river's breast.

Yet woman's step hath hastened
Along the reedy side,
And here, this very morn, a draught,
Drawn from the fount of life, is quaffed
   And thirst is satisfied.

Listen! The air is throbbing
As with a life new-born:
And Europe's echoes, to proclaim
The sweetness of a Saviour's name,
   Have wakened up this morn.

There came a stranger herald
From o'er the purple sea,
And on his eager lips he bore
Tidings for Europe's farthest shore,
Life from the dead for evermore—
Light, gladness, victory!

Behold yon group reclining
Amidst the bending reeds!
Think ye that woman's brow ere caught
Such broad expanse of holy thought
From Hellas' fable-creeds?

Think ye that any tidings,
Save those of deathless grace,
Could ever light her heavenward eye
With such a sudden radiancy?—
As if some angel, passing by,
Had smiled upon her face;

And she had smiled in answer,
With glad, yet calm surprise,
The while a casket, locked and sealed,
Had straightway opened, and revealed
A wondrous pearl of price.

Daughter of Thyatira!
Thy soul hath found her quest!
The pearl thou ne'er couldst find enrolled
Amongst earth's purple and her gold,
This very morn — unbought, unsold —
Is clasped upon thy breast!

Christ's chariot-wheels of conquest
Roll not with pomp and din:
The Spirit breathes — and straightway part
The yielding portals of her heart,
And Jesus enters in.

His name, like fragrant incense,
With prayer and praise is blent :—
The great Apostle's living word
This morn the pulse of life hath stirred,
Of a new continent!*

---

* Saint Paul's preaching at Philippi is the first historical record of the proclamation of the Gospel in Europe.

JEPHTHAH'S DAUGHTER,

JUDGES, CHAP. XI.

> "The daughter of the warrior Gileadite;
> A maiden pure, as when she went along
> From Mizpeh's towered gate, with welcome light,
> With tabret and with song."—TENNYSON.

By cedar mount and by cypress glen
Hath passed the tramp as of armèd men;
And Minnith's ripened sheaves were crushed,
And the vintage-bowers of Heshbon flushed
      Deep red — but not with wine!
And the priests of Chemosh looked aghast,
And the idols quaked as the troop swept past,

And the battled gates of Aroer reeled ;
And, on splintered lance and dinted shield,
  The tears of morning shine.

And the Gileadite, with a weary hand,
Hath wiped the gore from his reeking brand ;
And with fierce, glad eye, and haughty brow,
He hath looked tow'rds heaven and read a vow
  He vowed before the fight.
With haughty brow and defiant eye
He reads that vow in the arching sky.
Warrior ! why start at the crimson glow ?
It was but the morning's ruddy flow
  Which poured that blood-red light !

O'er Arnon's stream, and by Jabbok's ford,
Ebbed the host of Jephthah and the Lord :
From silent shrine, and from wailing town,
Where the pride of Ammon lies smitten down,
  Like a reed before the gale.

By cedar mount and by cypress glen,

Rolled back the tramp as of armèd men,

Till the balmy gales of Gilead swell

The floating banners of Israel,

    Amid her olives pale.

Amid her olives pale—near Mizpeh's tower—
Hiding her sweetness—droops a lily flower,
Waiting the warrior's coming smile ;—as pause
Spring-buds for summer, ere they ope their vase
And pour forth perfume.—Jephthah's only child
Had grown amongst the lilies of the wild,
By the same sunlight nectar-stored as they,
By the same dewdrops nurtured day by day,
By the same balmy breezes softly fanned,
Till seemed she sister of the lily band.
Sister—yet queen!—so stately towered her stem!
So royally hath beauty's diadem
Touched her young brow!—too soft, too childlike yet
To bear the crown with all its diamonds set!

The wildwood knew her footstep. The gazelle
Would stand and watch her at the palmy well,
Dipping her pitcher — with his soft, wild eye
Resting on hers. The bulbul would reply
To the rich, flute-like warble of her note,
With his best trill, before his voice could float
Over the maiden's. From the fragrant myrtle,
When her light step danced past, the brooding turtle.
Bridling its neck, would coo, in gentle swells,
A welcome to the dancer's timbrel bells.
And when, at eve, oft bent her listening ear
To catch her sire's proud footfall drawing nea
Leaning to meet him from the rude verandah,
Amidst the trellis of the oleander,
The fire-flies glanced, as if in fond caresses,
O'er the soft braidings of her ebon tresses.

Thus grew she. And her sire — that haughty man,
Whose brow had burned beneath the exile's ban,

Well nigh forgot, charmed by her soft control,
That the hot iron e'er had scorched his soul.
Like a tall cedar by the lightning scarred,
With a stern fate his strong will grappled hard,
And waved defiance to the tempest's wing,
And budded fresh at breathing of the spring,
And spread his boughs to catch the dewdrops sweet,
To filter o'er the lily at his feet!

But mute the timbrel bells, and hushed the dance,
And troubled grew her forehead's smooth expanse,
(Like rippling lake, just ere the threads of mist
Have wove the storm-cloud, and the breeze hath kissed
Its surface, leaving still its depths unstirred)
When stooped she, like a willowy reed, to gird
Her father's sword upon his thigh, and shook
The dust from off his plume. One long, long look —
And he was gone! The lily closed her urn
With the sun's setting — till his beams return.

" When will he come ?   I've searched the glowing east,
With gaze as earnest as the sun-god's priest
Watching for morning.   With an aching eye,
I've swept the fiery arch of southern sky,
Yet hailed no glint of lance, no corselet's glare,
No snow-white pennon floating in the air.
I've hearkened for the victor-song, until
My fancy heard it in the gushing rill,
And voice of bird, and harping touch of breeze
Sweeping the branches of the mulberry trees !
When will the conqueror come ?   No mighty foe,
Oh, warrior Gileadite ! could lay *thee* low ;
No Gentile arm could draw the fatal sword
Against the strength of Jephthah—and the Lord !

" But, hark !   'Twas *not* the voice of gushing stream,
Nor bird, nor breeze !   'Twas *not* the noontide's gleam
On silvery birch-stems !—nay ! I know that song !
I know those pennons as they stream along !

I know that plume which waves above the lines,
Like a tall cedar midst a grove of pines!
I know that choral air! No gentile tongue
Hath e'er profaned its holiness, or flung
Its glory o'er *their* banners. Egypt's sea
Once moaned its echo. Listen! ' *Gloriously*
The Lord hath triumphed!' Hush!—It dies away!
Breathe low, O summer wind! Thy treble stay,
O shrill-voiced bird! Again the swelling strain
Reaches its higher notes,—' *The Lord shall reign*
For ever and for ever!'

" Maidens sweet!
Come forth, with timbrel and with dance, to meet
The mighty man of valour! Nay, sweet singers!
Draw back one moment! Let his daughter's fingers
Sound his first welcome! Let *my* step alone
Dance forth to meet him, o'er his threshold stone!
Forgive my boldness!— he hath only me!

‘ Sing to the Lord, who triumphed gloriously !
The horse and rider He hath thrown — hath thrown !'

" My father ! Oh, my father !"

       But a groan
Brake from that strong man's breast — as if Despair
Kept his fell court, and shook his sceptre there !
And the broad cedar quivered 'neath her clasp,
Like a reed shaken in the tempest's grasp.

" My father ! Oh, my father ! My embrace
Hath troubled thee ! Perchance thy daughter's face
Hath lost its roselight — through the long, long yearning,
And lonely vigil, for my sire's returning ?
Ah, thou wilt hail the roselight flowing back.
In a swift current o'er thy homeward track !
What mean these words so hollow, faint, and slow —
' Alas, my daughter ! thou hast brought me low ?'

Thy lips *once* breathed, but *only once*, till now,
Such greeting. Fifteen springs agone, when thou
Wept o'er a new-born babe (a wailing thing!)
Who crossed, upon life's threshold, the white wing
Of 'parting mother—*then* thou whisperedst slow
' Alas, my daughter! thou hast brought me low!'
(So said they.) 'Twas but once. And since that hour
Thou hast poured forth upon thy child such dower
Of love so rich, I deemed the golden ore
Would last my lavish need for evermore!"

The maiden paused. Then, suddenly, her plaint
(The sobbing voice, subdued, and low, and faint,)
So changed; that they who wept the while they listened.
Stood breathless. And a strange, wild glory glistened
On her expanded brow,—*now* firm to bear
The beauty-crown, with every diamond there!
No longer, now, a frail and trembling vine,
Throwing her tendrils round the Strong to twine,

At her full height she rose, sublime and calm.
Erect, majestic, as the stately palm.

" Father ! Shall Jephtha's daughter dare withhold.
From the Lord's work, the silver and the gold,
The onyx and the jacinth ? Without falter
Thy lamb shall come, unsmitten, to the altar :
And yield, unbound, untethered, her young life,
Bending her neck to meet the slayer's knife.
If thou have oped thy mouth unto the Lord.
Do with thy child according to thy word !
One boon I crave. The firstling lamb is parted.
A little season from the joyful-hearted,
Ere it be subject to the priestly eyes,
And sealed, as spotless, for the sacrifice.
Part me from *thee*, my Father ! from all bands
That draw me *down*,— not *upward!*—all that stands
Eclipsing Heaven from earth ! And ere I die.
Let me bewail my young life's elegy

On the lone mountains; till, amidst that wail,
Heaven's sponsal hymn of love my virgin heart may hail

* * * * * *

* * * * *

The oleander wildly grew, untrimmed,
Around a voiceless home. The bulbul hymned
His song, without a rival. The gazelle
Waited and wondered, at the palmy well.
The turtle stretched her neck, but breathed no answer
To tuneful timbrel, or to timbrel dancer.

The storm-clouds, on the bleak and lonely mountains,
Drew back their shadows. And the torrent fountains
Poured silvery cadences; as Gilead's daughters
Wove their sweet wailings with the voice of waters.
And ever and anon a choral key
Burst from their Leader so exultingly,
All other voices paused in breathless wonder,
And brake their sad elegiac bands in sunder,

And strained their quavering voices hopelessly,
To reach the glory of their Leader's key.

Heaven's angels marvelled, as they swept their strings,
And domed the mountain with their radiant wings,
Sheltering the maiden's head.   Perchance the haze,—
The dim, wild twilight of her early days,—
Had parted : and she glimpsed the life immortal,
And the SIN OFFERING, ready at the portal!

ELIEZER AT THE FOUNTAIN.

GENESIS, CHAP. XXIV.

'Twas the golden hour of sunset,
  When the palm beside the well
Waveth o'er the fainting lilies;
And the desert amaryllis
  Shutteth up its crimson bell.

'Twas the hour when myrrh and cassia
  Drop their fragrant tears of balm;
And when Padan-aram's daughters
Come to draw the cooling waters,
  From the well beneath the palm.

ELIEZER AT THE FOUNTAIN.

Who art thou, O Syrian stranger!
With that meekly-thoughtful brow?
Heeding not the cool breeze, stealing
Softly o'er thy camels, kneeling
   'Neath the palm-tree's feathery bough;

With their thirsty nostrils quivering
To inhale the fountain's breath;
And the patient eyes, soft glistening;
And the drooping ears quick-listening
   To the bubbling sound beneath!

Calm, and motionless, and viewless,
Though his lips be seen to move,
Stands that Stranger,—and converses
With a viewless Fount of mercies,—
   With a living Well of love.

Ah! that lofty heavenward vision,
And that brow, sublimed with thought,

Be not of the earth's poor moulding,
Nor of nature's own unfolding,
 But from holier impress caught.

He hath washed the feet of Angels,
While the reverent knee he bent;
He hath spread the banquet lowly,
For the heavenly and the holy,
 By his master's desert tent.

He hath seen a lordly heirship
Court his grasp,—yet pass him by;
He hath viewed the wild flower blossom
On the bondmaid's swarthy bosom,
 Flushed with pride; nor heaved a sigh.

He hath hailed the Angel-message,
Without mockery or scorn;

And hath added his poor blessing
To the Princess*-wife's caressing,
   When the seed elect was born.

   He hath watched the child of promise
   Flourish like the cedar's bough ;
Yea! and *shuddered*, as he noted
A mysterious cloud that floated
   O'er his master's reverent brow ;

   When they left the well of Sheba,
   Early at the blink of day,
And turned northward, to Moriah,
With the wood — the knife — the fire —
   But no firstling lamb to slay!

   He hath hailed the home returning ;
   And hath marked on either face,

---

* " Sarah," in the Hebrew, signifies " Princess."

A strange joy ; a holy sweetness ;
As of men who *proved* the meetness,
And the glory and completeness
   Of the covenant of grace.

Now behold, on trustful mission,
   (Vowed in truth,—in faith obeyed,)
Just ere Padan-aram's daughters
Came to draw the limpid waters,
   He hath reached the palm-tree's shade.

Wafted like a breath of incense,
   Heavenward flew his wingèd thought ;
Yea! and there was incense blending
With the prayer to heaven ascending,
   From a holier censer caught.

Ere the whispered prayer was uttered,
   It was registered on high ;

Almost ere the words were spoken,
Almost ere he asked the token,
   Lo! the answer draweth nigh!

Drawing nearer,— brighter,— clearer,
   Bethuel's daughter comes in sight,
With her pitcher on her shoulder;
Just as sunset rays enfold her
   In a golden web of light.

Not the brightest maids of Hellas,
   By the blue Ægean sea,
Pressing forth the vine's rich juices —
Not the sweetest of the Muses,
   Dipping draughts from Castaly,—

Not the fairest nymph in Tempe,
   With her urn and chorded shell,—

Match this maiden, standing queenly,
Yet so meekly and serenely,
  'Neath the palm beside the well;

In that grand and Eve-like beauty,
Ere the tides of nations crossed,
And the dark world's ruth and evil
Crushed the Eden-type primeval,
  And the shattered fragments lost.

"Drink, my lord!" In limpid sweetness,
Soft, and angel-like, and clear,
Through the golden ether fluttered
Every syllable she uttered,
  Like rich music to his ear.

"Drink, my lord! and for thy camels
Let me draw the while they drink!"

Oh, each accent that was spoken
Only wrought the outward token
  Of prayer answered, link by link!

  Soon the maiden of the fountain
  Lit the patriarch's tent with joy!
Soon the Padan-aram lily
Drank the waters, pure and stilly,
  Of the sweet well Lahai-roi!

THE BETTER CHOICE.

MOAB OR ISRAEL?—*Ruth* i.

The glorious summer sun of Palestine
   Was ripening harvests to a paler gold,
And swelling the rich clusters of the vine,
   In Hebron's gardens, in the days of old;

When on the hills of Moab paused and stood
   Three wayfarers — and each, across her breast,
Folded the dusky robe of widowhood,
   In silence — as with speechless woe opprest.

One looked as though the heavy hand of time
   Had given weight to sorrow; but the twain
Were beautiful in womanhood's sweet prime:
   Too new to grief the dregs of woe to drain!

The aged mourner, when she raised her eye
  From the rough splinters of the craggy fell,
Looked ever *westward*—where in gladness lie
  The balmy vales of blessèd Israel.

One youthful mourner, ever and anon,
  Turned *eastward*—where the flocks of Moab feed,
And blithe young shepherds, to the torrent's moan,
  Gave back the music of the hollow reed.

The *other* neither looked to east nor west—
  Nor back on Moab, nor on Hebron's vale:
But folded her young arms across her breast,
  And *heavenward* turned her brow, serene and pale.

What saw she in the broad and blue expanse,
  That brought the flush back to her tear-stained face?
Why stands she, rapt as in some holy trance,
  Bathing her forehead in the fount of grace?

Hath Faith unrolled the secret scroll of time,
    And shown the plucking of a wild, green shoot
From Moab's stock—nursed in a heathen clime,
    And grafted into Israel's chosen root;

Stretching forth branches, wet with heavenly dew,
    From the sweet vales of hallowed Bethlehem;
'Till, on her topmost bough, all glorious, grew
    The "*Righteous Branch*" from David's royal stem?

We know not—but she stood like one whose feet
    Are planted on a Rock which ne'er shall move;
Girding her heart with high resolve, to meet
    The aged mourner's farewell words of love.

" Turn!—Turn again!—each to thy father's house
    Each to thy country's bowers of joy and light:
Each to the bridal train, the loving vows,
    The wedded truth of some young Moabite!

" Turn back, my daughters!—Dwell where ye have dwelt :
    Under the fruitage of the household vine.
The Lord deal kindly with you, as ye dealt
    Kindly with me—and with your dead, and mine!"

They lifted up their voices—and they weep!
    Tears! ye be precious as the costliest pearls—
Or, as the transient dews of morning, cheap,
    Which the next zephyr into sunshine whirls.

Both daughters wept!—*One* turned! Oh, human love!
    'Tis a frail tether which thy fibres twine.
Unless the thread they spin be interwove
    With the immortal cord of love divine!

Back to her country, and her childhood's haunts!
    Back to the wayside brooks, the glad abodes!
Back to the battled tower, the song, the dance!
    Back to her people, and her people's gods!

There paused *two* wayfarers on Moab's hills —
   List to that voice which cleaves the liquid air,
With low soft pleadings, falling in sweet trills;
   Strong in resolve, while meek in lowly prayer!

" Entreat me not to leave thee, nor to turn
   From following thee! Where thou dost go, I go :
Where thou dost dwell, I dwell : and meekly learn
   No other people but the Lord's to know.

" Where thou dost die, I die : and sleep beneath
   The balmy dews on Israel's hallowed sod.
Naught shall divide us, save the hand of death!—
   Naught part us —*for thy God shall be my God!*"

Two weary travellers, one eve, came down
   From Moab's hills. They thread the olive dell,
And pass the cornfields, to the little town —
   Stopping to drink at Bethlehem's cooling well.

THE GLEANER.

Ruth, chap. ii.

Oh, the harvest fields of Bethlehem!
    How beauteous to behold
The nodding ear, and the rustling stem,
    And the wavy sea of gold!

And the sharpened sickle's flashing glint,
    And the reapers, strong and blithe,
And the harvest flowers of many a tint,
    And the gleaners, young and lithe!

Oh, the owner of that goodly land,
    A thankful man was he,
When he stood amidst the reaper band,
    And blessed the company:

And when his servant's benison
    Benignly he receives,
As he looks around, and passes on,
    Amongst the yellow sheaves;

Calling to mind the harvest's Lord,
    And what He spake of yore,
In many a gracious, loving word,
    For the stranger and the poor.*

But who is she that bendeth low,
    With cheek so fair and pale,
Folding across her youthful brow
    The widow's dusky veil;

Pacing, with earnest step serene,
    'Till noon, from early morn,
Down stooping patiently to glean
    The scattered ears of corn?

---

* See Leviticus, xix. 6, and Deut. xxiv. 19. &c.

She never turns to join the laugh
    Of the merry Hebrew maid,
Nor stops the cooling urn to quaff,
    Beneath the plantain shade.

The highborn, Israelitish girl,
    With dark and flashing eye,
Her haughty lip with scorn may curl,
    And pass the stranger by.

The stranger's heart is communing
    With One whose ways are just;
Beneath the shadow of whose wing
    The friendless came to trust;

Leaving the bower of childhood's mirth,
    Leaving the natal sod,
For one poor, lonely widow's hearth,
    And for that widow's God:

Grasping His mighty arm, unseen.
    In weakness and in blindness,
And willing trustfully to lean
    Upon His loving-kindness.

" My mother! let me go, I pray,
    And glean thee bread to eat;
Mayhap thy God will bless my way,
    And guide my doubtful feet."

Forth went she while the dews of morn
    Still lay, in sparkling gems,
Upon the nodding ears of corn,
    And on the rustling stems.

She happed upon a field to light,
    Which bore a kinsman's name;—
Who led thee there, young Moabite?—
    The God of Abraham!

'Twas He, who with His touch of grace
    The rich man's soul did move,
To look upon the stranger's face
    With kindness and with love.

Oh, joy! with ephah full of grain,
    When evening shadows fell,
Again to cross the olive plain,
    And drink at Bethlehem's well:

And teach the widowed heart to bless
    Her God, for all His ways,
And change the robe of heaviness
    For the comely garb of praise!

THE LITTLE CAPTIVE MAID.

2 Kings, chap. v.

There dwelt beneath the pleasant shade
    Of fig-tree and of vine,
A little Israelitish maid,
    In holy Palestine.
It was a land of brooks and springs;—
    A land of corn and wine.

And, kinglike, o'er that watered vale,
    Proud Lebanon looked down,
In mantle fringed with lilies pale,
    And dusky cedar crown;
High in the purple dome of heaven
    Veiling his lordly frown.

I ween 'twas in a pleasant spot,
    This little maid did dwell ;
And softly round her father's cot
    The dews of blessing fell ;
I ween that in this home they loved
    The God of Israel.

She never bent the rebel knee
    'Neath Baal's mystic oak,
Nor bowed her head where, gloomily,
    His impious altars smoke.
She rested in Jehovah's smile,
    And wore His easy yoke.

But He, whose thoughts are not as ours,
    Had higher plans of grace,
And far away from Sharon's bowers,
    Appointed her a place,
Wherein her little lamp might shine
    Amidst a heathen race.

'Twas sunset;—and a flood of gold
    Had bathed the western fell;
The flocks were gathered to the fold,
    And watered at the well;
The turtle nestled o'er her brood,
    Far in the myrtle dell.

But hark!—The neigh of prancing steeds
    Bursts on the stilly air,
And, sweeping o'er the dewy meads,
    Is seen the corslet's glare;
And flash of sword, and glint of spear,
    Are marked defiling there.

O'er fold and field,—on bower and cot,
    War-horse and rider rushed;
The dewy breath of night grows hot,
    The vintage bowers lie crushed;
And, with the life-blood of the slain
    The trodden vines are flushed.

'Tis past!—The fierce marauding band
    Have sheathed the gory glaive,
And swiftly to the Syrian's land
    Rolled back the ebbing wave;
And the little maid of Israel
    Is captive and a slave!

They counted out the pieces bright
    Of silver and of gold;
They wrangled o'er the wrong and right,
    In voices harsh and bold;
And the little bondmaid's tears fell fast,
    As every piece was told.

In gilded cage the captive bird
    Forgets its woodland nest,—
The brooklet by the breezes stirred,—
    The mother's downy breast,—
The shady nook where, cool and clear,
    The pearly dewdrops rest.

But ne'er, I ween, this little maid
    Forgat the lowly cot,
Beneath the vine and fig-tree's shade,
    Where God was unforgot;—
I ween that from His holy law
    Her heart departed not.

And thrice a-day she open threw
    The lattice of her cell,
And turn'd her gentle face unto
    The land of Israel—
The land wherein her God had said
    His holy Name should dwell.

And thrice a-day she bent her knee,
    And ask'd her God to bless
The lowly bondmaid—and to be
    Strength to the fatherless—
A well-spring in a thirsty land,
    A rest in weariness!

She little knew, while, day by day,
    A lonely path she trod,
Her humble lamp should show the way
    That led to Israel's God;
And that the master, from the slave,
    Should learn this blessed road.

He was a valiant man of might,
    And round his princely head
Bright laurels, won in many a fight,
    Their glorious lustre shed;
And, in a nation's roll of fame,
    His honour'd name was read.

Yet, Syrian! what avails for thee
    The wreath, the monarch's smile,
While the dire plague of leprosy
    Thy beauty doth defile;
And the proud mien and stately brow
    Are all accounted vile?

There drops no balm in Syria's land,
 To heal thy fell disease —
No true Physician's potent hand,
 To bring thee health and ease!
Where be thy gods — thy mighty ones —
 Thy idol deities?

In vain, through Rimmon's temple, smokes
 The cloudy censer's breath —
In vain her impious priest invokes
 The name of Ashtoreth!
The only answer is a wail
 Of darkness, hell, and death!

" Oh would to God my master knew
 The prophet that doth dwell
Where softly falls the healing dew
 On favour'd Israel!
He serveth One, whose grace alone
 Can make the leper well!"

'Twas but the breathing of a thought —
    The whisper of a sigh —
And yet thy words, young captive, wrought
    God's will, so mightily,
That there was joy on earth below,
    And joy in heaven on high.

They yoke the chariot to the steeds;
    They form in glittering line;
They pass the brazen gate that leads
    Tow'rds holy Palestine; —
They cross the oleander plains,
    And climb the hills of pine.

And from the tall, pavilion'd tower
    Gazed forth that little maid —
Watching, through many a weary hour,
    The moving cavalcade —
Now argent in the glistening sun,
    Now darkening in the shade.

Perchance, with many a gushing tear
 Those gentle eyes were drown'd,
While thought she of the land so dear
 For which that train was bound;—
And she, like some uprooted flower,
 Left in a thirsty ground!

Alas! how many a weary night,
 On flagging wing, passed by!
How many a sunset bathed in light
 The glorious western sky!
And from the tall, pavilioned tower
 Still gazed that aching eye!

Hark!—'tis the roll of chariot-wheels,
 The voice of charioteer,
The courser's neigh, the shout, the peals
 Of jubilee and cheer!
And Pharpar and Abana curl,
 In joy, their ripples clear.

The brazen gate is open swung,
    With welcome and acclaim;
The lattice-shades are backward flung
    By many a Syrian dame;
And round the wayworn chariot-wheels
    Men bow, in low salaam!

And in that chariot standeth one
    Upon whose radiant face
New life, new health, new youth have shone;
    And where beholders trace
A *strange* expression—beautiful
    With more than nature's grace!

A beauty and a light, ne'er caught
    From Rimmon's lying creed!—
A solemn grandeur, never wrought
    Of any mortal deed;—
A bloom and goodliness ne'er sprung
    From any earthly seed!

Oh! he hath found the lowly place
    Where healing waters roll;
And he hath reached the Fount of grace
    Which cures the leprous soul;
And he hath ventured in, and proved
    That faith can make him whole.

In Jordan dwelt no virtue rare,
    No healing power divine;
(The Syrian streams flowed pure and fair
    As those of Palestine)—
It was the blood of Christ which cleansed,
    And Jordan was the sign.

The finger of a little child
    The way to healing showed;
'Twas a poor bondmaid's light which smiled
    Upon that heavenward road:
For there are none too weak—too poor—
    To point the way to God!

And she who pined for Sharon's bowers —
　　The sweet, uprooted rose —
Soon opened wide faith's budding flowers.
　　Where light immortal glows : —
Transplanted to a holier land,
　　Where milk with honey flows!

MISCELLANEOUS.

RUNNYMEDE.

'Twas not in hostile phalanx,
  To face some foreign foe,
With spear, and sword, and crested helm,
  And battle-axe and bow,
That the barons of old England
  Each reined his panting steed,
And the British lion shook his mane
  On the field of Runnymede!

No strife for empty glory
  Draws here the glittering brand;
No battle this for ownership
  O'er a few roods of land;

No struggle for inscribing.
  With blood, a hollow name ;
No fight to win a narrow space
  In the musty rolls of fame ;
But a nation's holy compact
  For liberty and right :
The British lion *will* be free,
  And who dare chain his might ?
Free as the foamy surges
  That lash his ancient rocks ;
Free as the chainless winds that root,
  In storms, his rugged oaks ;
Free as the monarch eagle
  That soars o'er northern mountains ;
Free as the thousand sparkling streams
  That leap from granite fountains !

From many a wall-girt city,
  From many a stately hall,

From many a stern baronial tower,
   With crenellated wall ;
From the orchard lands of Devon,
   From the moorlands of the North,
From Severn unto royal Thames,
   The gallant band rode forth.

From where Northumbria's castles
   Frown o'er the surging deep ;
From where, on meres of Westmorland,
   The mountain shadows sleep ;
From southern wolds and forests,
   Where wild deer loved to dwell,
And waving harvests gild the field
   Where Saxon Harold fell :
Came many a Norman baron,
   Each with his knightly train,
And many a noble Saxon earl,
   And many an ancient thane :

And, in its jewelled scabbard,
    Was hid the polished brand;
And stainless banners proudly waved
    In many a strong right hand.

Men, whom dark deadly hatreds
    Had riven long asunder,
Who met not, save, as in the sky,
    Meet lurid clouds of thunder,
Here pledged their haughty greetings,
    And side by side upstood;
And grasped each other's steel-gloved hand,
    In common brotherhood.
Brave Saxon and proud Norman
    Here own *one* stubborn creed—
For a craven king, against his will,
    Keeps tryst at Runnymede!
And ere the golden sunlight,
    Which rose this morn, go down,

A shower of false mock pearls shall fall
  From a recreant monarch's crown;
And the baldric that shall girdle
  His ermined robe of state,
Shall be fastened with a stronger clasp
  Than a people's fear and hate.

They chose for council chamber,
  No dimly lighted room,
With gold-emblazoned throne of state,
  And purple-broidered dome;
But the sapphire roof of heaven,
  With its sunlight, free and broad;
And the broidered carpet that they pressed
  Was England's dewy sward!
And the ancient river rippled
  A smile while flowing on;
And the summer breeze, in the old oak trees,
  Whispered a benison!

Then stood forth bold Fitzwalter,*
  In his steel-wrought coat of mail;
And proudly, slowly lifted up
  His barrèd aventayle.
And on his polished hauberk
  His sheathèd sword did ring,
The while, with steady pace, he strode
  Right towards the craven king.

Robed in his crimson tunic,
  With costly jewels set,
And girdled with his golden belt,
  Sat John Plantagenet.
The crown of England tottered
  Upon his crispèd curls;
And his mantle waved in silken folds,
  Clasped with a brooch of pearls.

* William Fitz-Walter, the Leader of the Barons.

Now speed thee, brave Fitz-Walter!
  Thou graspest in thine hand
A nobler weapon than the blade
  Of thy good Damascus brand;
Thy roll of lettered parchment
  May soil, but ne'er decay;
Thy children's children bless thee still
  For what thou held'st that day!

He knelt, in mute obeisance,
  Upon his mailèd knee.—
And a fresh breeze wakened, and unrolled
  The Charter of the Free!
And a golden sunbeam, falling
  On the ebon and the white,
Made luminous the characters,
  As with a sudden light.

Then paled the King with fury,
  And gnashed his teeth with rage,

The while his quivering eye glanced down
    That mighty parchment's page.
And the grey goose-quill did flutter
    Within his trembling hand,
As, like a cruel pard at bay,
    His stubborn foes he scanned.
But he saw that every scabbard
    Contained a trusty sword;
And he saw a band of sturdy squires,
    Around each feudal lord;
And a troop of stalwart yeomen,
    To back each valiant knight,
With cross-bow, spear, and battle-axe,
    All ready armed for fight;—
So he signed the "MAGNA CHARTA:"
    And the royal signet set
On the sole good deed that was ever done
    By John Plantagenet!

And the banner of old England
    Waved proudly from that hour;

And baron, earl, and knight, and squire,
  Spurred back to hall and tower;
Where many a highborn lady
  Kept vigil for her lord,
And waited many a fair-haired girl
  To loose her father's sword.

I ween 'twas joy to listen,
  (When, round the winter's fire,
The matron wrought her tapestry,
  And the daughter touched her lyre,)
To the father's stirring story
  Of the noble band that met,
And fought, and won the bloodless fight
  'Twixt crown and coronet.
The strong old tower shall totter,
  The young oaks shall decay,
But, from the field of Runnymede,
  No glory pass away.

Now hail to the mighty Charter,

    The heirloom of the Free!

And hail to the flag of the Island Queen.

    That waves o'er land and sea!

And hail to each British Mother

    Who nurtures boys as bold,

—*Yet gentler*—than the sturdy band,

    In the good, brave days of old!

" As this was the first effort towards a legal governmen
so is it, beyond comparison, the most important event i
our history, except the Revolution: without which its ben
fits would have been rapidly annihilated. The Constitutio
of England has, indeed, no single date from which its de
rivation is to be reckoned. The institutions of positive la
the far more important changes which time has wrought i
the order of society, during 600 years subsequent to th
great Charter, have undoubtedly lessened its direct appl
cation to our present circumstances. But it is still *t/
keystone of English liberty.* All that has since been obtaine
is little more than a confirmation or commentary; and
every subsequent law were to be swept away, there woul
still remain the bold features that distinguish a free fro

a despotic monarchy. It has lately been the fashion to depreciate the value of "Magna Charta," as if it had sprung from the private ambition of a few selfish Barons, and redressed only some feudal abuses. . . . An equal distribution of civil rights to *all classes* of freemen forms the peculiar beauty of the Charter."— HALLAM, *Middle Ages*, vol. ii., p. 446.

PHILIPPINA WELSER.

A FEW miles from Innsbruck, on the road to Salzburg, stands the battlemented castle, " Schloss Ambras," the ancient residence of the Archdukes of the Tyrol. Many an old historic memory peoples its dismantled halls; but the one single episode which endears the place is the embalmed memory of the fair Philippina Welser, the wife of Ferdinand, Count of Tyrol, son of the Emperor Ferdinand I. She is still the ideal genius of the place. " Whose was this old virginal, so carefully kept, and duly dusted?" " Philippina Welser's!" " Whose this little, quaint work-box, with its rusty tambour needles and bodkins?" " Philippina Welser's!" " Whose work was that piece of faded embroidery?" " Philippina Welser's!" " Whose was that suit of armour?" " Ferdinand's, the husband of Philippina Welser?" " Whose chamber is this? whose oratory?" " Philippina Welser's!" " But who was Philippina herself?" " She was the most beautiful woman of her time; the sweetest and the best: the daughter of a simple citizen of Augsburgh." " But how did she become an Archduchess? and how came she here?" " There was a Diet of the Empire at Augsburgh, in 1550; and the young Ferdinand, then only nineteen, caught sight of the beautiful girl, and loved her. She was not lightly won. But, at last, they were secretly married, and Ferdinand brought his bride here, to his hereditary castle, where they lived together in rare, connubial happiness, for thirty-one years. The old Kaiser was furious at his son's *mésalliance;* and, for eight years, would listen to no entreaty for reconciliation. But the same beauty, which had once charmed the son to love, at length charmed the father to forgiveness. One day, a beautiful stranger, leading a princely boy in either hand, threw herself at the Emperor's feet, and claimed and gained his parental love.

"Philippina, rose of Augsburgh!
    Blooming on thy stem, alone!
Wherefore turn thee from the homage
    Of thy noble Kaiser's son?"

"I am but a burgher's daughter,
    And the brow thou callest fair
Never fashioned was, nor moulded
    Ducal crown of pearls to wear.
Never have my maiden musings
    Stolen beyond my father's hall;

Plying swift my tambour needle,
    Playing soft my virginal!
And the wildest of my visions
    Was, beneath the matron coif,
To confine these vagrant tresses
    As a simple burgher's wife!
Thou, whose cradle was empanelled
    With the Double Eagle's wings;
And whose purple line hath mingled
    Ever with the blood of kings;—
All *thy* visions should be lofty;
    Soaring proud,—as eagles sail:—
All *my* thoughts are meek and lowly;
    Like the cushat's of the vale.
Turn thee to the Kaiser-palace:—
    Seek some noble, lily hand:—
Some fair bride, whose high aspirings
    Throb with thine, brave Ferdinand!
Nay! I know what thou would'st answer:
    Yet this face thou callest bright,

And these locks thou stylest golden,
   Soon must lose their bloom and light.
How will, then, the crown archducal
   Grace a brow of faded bloom?
Tell me: will the 'rose of Augsburgh'
   Never lose her first perfume?
Now, she blushes in youth's morning;
   And the dew is in her cup.—
Listen! Soon the breath of noontide
   Will have scorched her beauty up.
Then, perchance, the pale rose, withered,
   Will be flung away—to die"—

But the noble blood of Hapsburg
   Flushed his cheek and fired his eye,
And he rose, erect, before her;
   And he leaned upon his brand:—
" By this good sword of my fathers,
   And the word of Ferdinand,

Not thy grace, nor bloom, nor beauty,
   —Angel-passing though they be,—
Could have won my loyal homage,
   Or have bent this mailèd knee!
These are but the crystal casket,
   And the jewel, shining through,
Will outlast the shivered crystal,
   Beautiful, immortal, true!
Let the diamond, first and purest,
   In my father's ' kaiser-kron,'
Weighed against this matchless jewel,
   Lightly, to the winds be thrown!
Philippina! Sweetest! Dearest!
   Wear, for *me*, the matron coif:
And forget the wreath archducal
   In the bosom-friend and wife."

So she oped the jewel-casket,
   And she tendered him her love.

And the bridal flowers were gathered,
 And the bridal veil was wove.
And he led her to his castle,
 In the valley of the Inn;
Where a guard of giant mountains
 Girdled her from strife and din.
And her goodness and her beauty
 Lighted up the gloomy pile,
To the gladness of a palace;—
 To the glow of summer's smile!

Dark the angry flush that passes,
 Slowly, o'er the Kaiser's face:
" Never will I own as daughter
 Maiden of the burgher race!
Never yet hath shield been quartered,
 With the proudly plumèd wings
Of the empire's Double Eagle
 But from ancient line of kings!"

So she meekly bowed to duty,
    Gladdened by her consort's love;
While she charmeth grief to gladness
    Wheresoe'er her footsteps move.
Lightening every peasant's burden
    With her bounty and her grace:
Bending o'er her babies' cradle,
    Angel-like, her radiant face.

    *   *   *   *   *

    *   *   *   *

Who is this, O haughty Kaiser!
    Matron-like, yet passing fair,
Blushing, like the almond's blossom,
    Midst a cloud of golden hair?
With a boy of princely bearing,
    Left and right, on either side,
Like the royal house of Hapsburg,
    (Curling lip, and eagle-eyed!)
Kneeling low, and kneeling lowly;
    Pleading soft, in broken tone,

"Kaiser! let me call thee *'Father!'*
  Bless the children of thy Son!"

Like the passing of a shadow
  From some Alpine peak of snow,
At the rosy kiss of sunshine,
  O'er his brow there came a glow,
Warm, as in our life's young morning;
  And he pressed her to his heart;
Whisp'ring,—" Deign to be my daughter;
  Angel-spirit though thou art!"

Did she linger in the palace,
  Blazing like a star of light,
With the pearly crown archducal
  Sparkling on her forehead bright?
Nay! the fortress of her early
  Wedded life of quiet love,
(Where the bridal veil was folded,
  And the matron coif was wove;

Where the cradle of her babies
    Glowed with many an Eden-thought,—
Bud, and fruit, and bird, and blossom,
    By her tambour needle wrought,)
There the home is, where her spirit
    Nestled lowly,—love-secure;
Midst the honour of the humble
    And the homage of the poor;
'Till the angels came to take her,
    Long before the shades of even,
To the pearl gates of a city,
    Where her heart found rest—and Heaven!

A GOOD-FRIDAY LEGEND.

A.D. 33.

"Old things are passed away."

Plutarch mentions a tradition, according to which, at the hour of the Saviour's agony, a wailing cry, like the dying of the false gods, swept across land and sea, in the hearing of certain mariners: *and so the oracles ceased.*

A MAIDEN of the classic South,
 In regions fancy-haunted,
Sang a wild story—half in truth,
But half the mythic dream of youth;—
 And thus her tale she chaunted.

"The helm was shipped,—the sail unbraced,
　　At daylight's rosy dawning;
And o'er the rippling waves he chased
　　The footsteps of the morning.

"I heard the lapping of the tide,
　　Down in the glen of myrtles,
Where he had lingered at my side
　　To listen to the turtles.

"With oar, and sail, and fisher's net,
　　His buoyant barque was freighted:—
'Twould bear him back ere Phœbus set,
　　Unless he were belated.

"I heard the Nereid's merry shout,
　　Within their oozy hollow;
I saw them dip and plunge about
　　His nimble boat to follow.

" The sea-green Oceanides
  Were joining in their laughter;
And, floating o'er the crimsoned seas,
  Were trooping blithely after.

" I danced upon the pebbly beach;
  I sang with wildered pleasure;
For well I knew they could not reach
  My own betrothèd treasure.

' I turned me to the ilex grove;
  Where dews were round me weeping;
And in a bower the shadows wove
  I caught the Dryads sleeping.

" They slept like tranced, insensate things,
  That ne'er expect a waking;
And then I heard the rush of wings,
  And felt a sudden shaking!

"I heard, beneath the white cascade,
  The reed-crowned Naiads splashing;
And started, in the laurel shade,
  At silvery pinions clashing.

"I marked a pale light through the gloom,
  But saw no clearer vision :—
It might have been mild Hermes' plume,
  On some Olympian mission.

"But just as evening's saffron train
  With night's dun vesture mingles,
I heard my fisher's barque again
  Upon the pebbly shingles.

"I sang my greeting clear and strong,
  But caught no tuneful answer;
I chaunted loud my sweetest song,
  But heard no choral stanza.

"Perchance it was the evening's chill
  Which dimmed that radiant forehead;
And sealed that lip, so pale and still,
  And blanched the cheek so florid.

"He brought no gift of ruby stem
  From ocean gardens floral;
Nor pearly shell, nor sparkling gem,
  Nor rosy frond of coral.

"We sat beneath an ancient pine,
  So weird, and scathed, and hoary;
And while I grasped his hand in mine,
  He told his wondrous story."

The Mariner's Story.

"'The helm was shipped,—the sail unbraced,
  At daylight's rosy dawning;

And o'er the rippling waves I chased
    The foosteps of the morning.

"' But soon there slowly, slowly fell,
    A hush o'er sky and ocean;
As if all nature owned one spell
    Of breathless, strange emotion.

"' The veilèd chariot of the sun
    Was darkened in high heaven,
Though scarcely yet three hours were run
    From noontide on to even.

"' The spirits of the air and sea
    All seemed to pause and languish:
Held in mysterious sympathy
    With some immortal anguish.

"' As though they watched, with love intense,
    Gasping, and wan, and breathless,

A fainting of Omnipotence —
    A dying of the deathless!

" ' The shores grew dim ; — the sweltering sky
    And moaning ocean darkened :
And then a voice came floating by,
    And I bowed down — and hearkened.

" ' It floated through unmeasured space,
    By distance undiminished ;
So awful — yet so full of grace
    It sounded — " IT IS FINISHED!"

" ' I heard Olympian palace-halls
    Slam home their ivory portals :
I heard the thyrsis as it falls
    From gasping, weird immortals.

" ' *Immortals?* Nay! a *mortal* cry
    Arose amid the silence ;

Answered by wails of agony,
   From sea, and shore, and islands.

"' From glen to cliff,— from bay to creek,
   A sobbing and a sighing;
From vale to mount, a wildered shriek
   As of the frore and dying!

"'*Finished!* Jove's palace-gates no more
   Will ope to hail the morrow:
I knew the age of dreams was o'er,
And the sweet Muses wept full sore,
   Yet felt I ruth nor sorrow.

"' Perchance there dawns a golden age,
   More bright than gilded trances;
When Truth shall ope a holier page
   Than poets' sweetest fancies.

"'Though bright Apollo ne'er again
    Shall mount his chariot golden,
His steeds will tramp that azure plain
    By mightier force upholden.

"'Though queenly Dian drop her bow
    Upon the dreamy mountain,
The moonlight still shall overflow
    Its silver-brimmèd fountain.

"'And spring's young flowers will bud and blush
    Without the breath of Flora;
And morning's rosy light outflush
    The fingers of Aurora.

"'The playful Nereids' winding shells
    Are hushed in hollow silence;
But Ocean's organ-voice still swells
    Around his caverned islands.

" ' And not a reed or flower will mourn
    One pleasant brook's cessation,
Though the sweet Naiad's broken urn
    Hath poured its last libation.

" ' And spirits blend in harmony,
    And love is strong for ever,
Though Cupid be a phantasy,
    And emptied be his quiver.

" ' Perchance there is a mightier Hand
    Than Jove's — to hold the thunder;
Perchance a kingly Throne shall stand,
    Though his be rent in sunder.

"*Ancient of Days*, — whose dateless morn
    Is timeless and eternal;
Elder than Chronos! — an Unborn,
    Whose Godhead is supernal.

"'*Finished!* The word was mystery;
 And clouds are intervening;
But faith is waiting for the key
 To comprehend its meaning.'"

AN OLD VERGER'S TALE.

When Queen Victoria visited Potsdam, in 1858, it happened that the old Verger, who showed her the tomb of Frederick the Great, was the same man who had showed the same shrine to Napoleon Buonaparte in 1805. When the Soldier-Emperor visited the Soldier's grave, the sword of the Dead was still kept as a national relic on the iron tomb. It was seized by the hand of Napoleon, and sent as a trophy of conquest to Paris; nor has it ever been restored to Prussia.

He placed his foot on that marble stone;
 The man whose name had passed
Over Europe, like the thunder's moan,
 And like the lightning's blast.
I heard the ring of his spur of steel,
 As, with quick and stubborn tread,
And folded arms, he set his heel
 By the tomb of our royal Dead.

The lamplight fell, as it falleth now,
    Through the chill of an autumn morn,
On his marble cheek and moveless brow,
    And chiselled lip of scorn.

I thought me, with a speechless dread,
    That the flags beneath me stirred;
But the tomb lay moveless o'er our Dead,
    And on the tomb — the sword!

We sighed no word, we raised no hand,
    When the Stranger's arm of fate
Stretched forth — and grasped the hilted brand
    Of the man we called "*The Great!*"

For the Prussian Eagle, in her woe,
    Forgat, one hour, her truth;
And her swarthy wing was drooping low,
    And her eye was dulled with ruth.

And the foeman triumphed! — for he saw
    The strong forget her might;
Loosening the orb from her left claw,
    And the sceptre from her right;

And a hundred thousand victors dashed
  Through our opened gates that day;
And a hundred thousand lances flashed,
  In long and bright array.
And banners streamed, and clarions blew,
  And the Gallic Eagle's wings
Were fluttering o'er a retinue
  Of false or subject kings.

Not long!—for the free Black Eagle rose
  In the strength of her ancient trust;
And she rent the banner of her foes,
  And dragged it through the dust.
And she burst the Frank's imperious chain,
  And his Eagles sped their flight;
For orb and sceptre were firm again
  In left claw and in right.

Aye! Fifty summers have come and flown.
  And we garnered in their sheaves;

And fifty autumns breathed their moan
    Among the withered leaves ;
And fifty times have the Christmas chimes
    Rung in new hope and trust,
Since that stubborn heel, with its spur of steel,
    Stood by our royal dust.

They said it once was joy to scan
    My boyhood's ringlets bright :—
You smile as you gaze on the bent old man,
    With his locks of snowy white.
Morn's orient tide,—noon's surging wave,
    Have flowed across my head ;
Yet still I watch by the soldier's grave,
    And pray by the kingly dead.
I have seen the glowing sunrise steep
    The floor with its crimson stain ;
I have watched the golden evening creep
    Adown that amber pane ;

I have marked the scutcheons' blazoned hues
    Grow pale and grey with time;
And I've seen the chiselled marbles lose
    The whiteness of their prime:
But I still kept vigil, as of yore,
    Amid the vaulted gloom,
When a Royal Stranger stood, once more,
    Beside our royal tomb.

She stood upon that self-same stone;—
    The Queen whose name hath passed
Around the world, like the dulcet tone
    Of a silver clarion's blast.
She stood,—with a hushed, yet queenly tread;
    In silence,—as in prayer:
With a drooping eye and a bending head,
    With its softly braided hair;
With lips which little babes have kissed,
    As cheek to cheek they lean;

And a brow where princely sons ne'er missed
    The *Mother*—in the *Queen*.
She wore no jewelled diadem,
    No ermine robe trailed she;
A woman's tear was her single gem,
    And her robe was charity.
No coat of mail, with its galling fold,
    Across her free heart pressed;
Her people's love is the shield of gold
    Which guards that queenly breast.

Oh happy isle where the roses smile
    Around her palace tower,
Where bloomed a rare sweet Bud to spare
    For the royal Prussian's bower!
We ask no sword on the Soldier's tomb,
    To keep our country free;—
The English Rose, with her true perfume,
    Our sweet defence shall be!

CHIMINGS.

The Beautiful and Dutiful!
   Oh rend them not in twain;
They be but sister links that hang
   Upon a golden chain.
The hand that rends the Beautiful
   From off its sister ring,
Will find, within its reckless grasp,
   A hollow, worthless thing.

The Beautiful and Dutiful,
   By balmy breezes fanned,
Through light and shade, unconsciously,
   Move heavenward, hand in hand:
They smile into each other's eyes,
   The while they pace along,

And exiles both from Paradise,
    They sing the Eden song.

The Beautiful and Dutiful!
    Oh, it is sweet to trace
Their work, in lovely unison,
    On gesture, form, and face.
The brow which grace is moulding fair,
    In Duty's gentle school,
Though bloom nor symmetry be there,
    Is passing beautiful!

The Youthful and the Truthful!
    Their bands should ne'er be riven;
For they were one in Edenland,
    And they are one in Heaven.
And every heart where Jesus dwells,
    — Himself the glorious " Truth,"—
Is watered by ten thousand wells
    Of fresh and fadeless Youth.

The Holy and the Lowly!
    No hand may dare to sever
The bond that binds them into one,
    For ever and for ever!
According to the heavenward pace
    At which the saint grows holy,
So, by the lamblike Saviour's grace,
    He groweth meek and lowly.

The Holy and the Lowly!
    They be not twain — but one;
Eternal their identity,
    And cannot be undone.
They be like Jacob's shining road,
    Wherein our faith can scan
Thy work, O holy Son of God,
    And lowly Son of man!

TO CECILIA.

'Tis said, in legendary lore,
By Tyber's bank dwelt one of yore
Who the sweet name thou bearest, bore.

Cecilia! And her brow was bright,
All radiant with celestial light,
Untouched by care, or stain, or blight!

And wheresoe'er she moved along,
The Angels, in a viewless throng,
Stooped down,— and listened to her song.

And as they shook the martyr's palm
Across her brow, sweet drops of balm
Fell there, and spread a holy calm.

And, now and then, an Angel's wing
Would sweep across some flagging string.
And wake a more ecstatic ring.

Whate'er the cadence of the tone,
They say the key-note was but one,
And this it was,—" *Thy will be done!*"

And thou, her namesake! on whose bloom
The shadowy palm of martyrdom
Will never cast its solemn gloom:

Thy lot it is to seek and find
The Beautiful with Truth combined;
And, serving God, to serve thy kind.

Life's common lessons can inspire
Tunes sweeter than the sweetest wire
That throbbed in Saint Cecilia's lyre.

When duties move in sweet accord,
And actions harmonise with word,
And thoughts lie subject to the Lord.

Thus, in thy daily life's routine,
Though clouds opaque may intervene,
Bright Angels watch thee, though unseen.

And when thou haltest in thy song,
And jarring notes rise high and strong,
In discord betwixt right and wrong;

Perchance the wafting of their wing
A cooling breath of life may bring
Across the jarred or broken string;

And tune it into song again,
Until thy spirit catch the strain,
And carry out the sweet refrain.

But soon the day shall dawn, when thou
Amidst the Angel-choir shalt bow,
With the saint's halo round thy brow:

Singing the anthem thou hast known
On earth, but in its feeblest tone,—
" *For ever, Lord, Thy will be done!*"

THE BABE AND THE SAINT.

We do not say, " Alas, how soon!" when, in morn's golden hour,
The folded, dewy bud bursts forth a bright and glorious flower;
We do not question, " Wherefore thus?" when borne on radiant wing,
The Psyche rises from its thrall, a living, glorious thing:
And yet how many a heavy sigh from aching bosoms broke,
When the Babe Katie fell asleep—and the Saint Katie woke!

Oh! Baby Katie was a sweet and winsome thing for earth!
A hundred happy smiles broke forth at tidings of her birth;
And trebled generations grouped to fondle earth's new guest;
And gentle arms have caught new skill in cradling her to rest:
And prayers have blent, at morn and eve, with glad thanksgiving strain,
Because the sweet Babe Katie comes to join the pilgrim train.

On right hand and on left, life's thorns were softly swept aside,
And Katie's teardrops, ere they fell, with kisses warm were dried;
And every grief was charmed away before it left its trace
Upon the placid sweetness of the dimpled baby face;

And flowers were wreathed, in festal guise, where'er
 she passed along;
And every smile was met with smiles, and every song
 with song!

It would not do! Those tender feet were never
 called to move,
Save o'er the jasper floor within the courts of
 heavenly love.
That small, soft hand was never framed to grasp the
 pilgrim staff;
That rosy lip was never meant from wayside brook to
 quaff;
Nor that sweet silvery voice to blend with any mortal
 hymn;—
Its tones be destined for the choir of waiting
 Seraphim!

What marvel, then, if Katie rose at golden peep of day,
Just tasted of the wayside brook, then sighed, and
 turned away?

What marvel if there shone a light within her earnest
    eye,
As if she saw the radiant wings of angels drawing
    nigh?
What wonder if there swept a shade across her infant
    brow,
As from the viewless wafting of a palm's victorious
    bough?

So the Babe Katie fell on sleep! The silver cord
    was riven!
But the Saint Katie wakened up! and there was joy
    in heaven!
And at the glorious melody of one victorious Name,
The gates of pearl, to let her in, flew back with glad
    acclaim;
And she hath learned to speak *that Name*,—to praise
    that untold grace,
Before her unknown Saviour's throne,—before her
    Father's face.

And doth she sometimes bend her down to scan that
    spot on earth,
Made beautiful for evermore by sweet Babe Katie's
    birth?
And doth she sometimes stoop, and breathe a voice-
    less whispering;
And fan her mother's pale sweet brow with soft and
    viewless wing;
And charm away that exile look of sorrow and of
    care:
And smile a golden beauty o'er that little lock of hair?

We know not! But we know that He, from whom
    the Child-gift came,
Who writ, within the book of life, the Saint's new
    heavenly name,
Will fill with gladness and with song the void and
    silent place,
And lighten up the darkness with the shining of His
    face;

'Till Sire and Mother bless their God, beneath the
chastening stroke,
For the Babe Katie, fallen asleep—and for the
Saint who woke!

A SABBATH REMINISCENCE.

We stood together, side by side,
    Sweet Eleanor and I.
Alas! a holier Sabbathtide,
    To her was drawing nigh.

With dulcet voice, subdued and calm,
    She read, in solemn tone,
The verses of the morning psalm,
    Alternate,— one by one.*

Her golden head was bent beneath
    The holy hush of prayer;
"Cast me not off!" The whispered breath
    Still seemed to linger there;

      * We were reading the 71st Psalm.

As if " old age" had nought to do
    With such a bud as this,
Whereon reposed life's morning hue
    Of softest, purest bliss.

The tender glow of mantling health
    Lay on her cheek of rose;
And in her eye love's hallowed wealth
    Was shrined, in meek repose.

I listened. O'er the psalmist's shell
    Lingered the same low tone;
" Forsake me not when strength shall fail!"
    Murmured that little one.

I marked her form of freest mould;
    The limbs so round and fair;
The shining locks, like thredded gold,
    Untouched by time or care.

What hath such prayer to do with *thee?*
    Young dream of joy and love!
Dear lute of sweetest melody,
    Tuned—but for courts above!

God heard her plea. The blight of age
    Ne'er breathed upon her bloom;
He willed not that earth's pilgrimage
    Should rifle heaven's perfume.

" Forsake me not!" The whispered prayer
    Soon reached the Father's throne;
Unstained by grief, undimmed by care,
    Jesus resumed *His own.*

She was but nine when she passed into the light of immortality, almost in the twinkling of an eye.

OUR DEPARTED TWAIN.

They were not mine, and yet my heart
  Caressed them as its own,
They seemed to bear so full a part
  In every sight and tone!
Their gladness seemed to blend its light,
  With every beam that shone.

I scarcely know what spell first bound
  My flowing tide of love,
To stay its sweep; and deepen round
  The bower thy childhood wove,—
Dear, rosy gift of summer joy!
  Dear, softly-pinioned dove!

A fountain was she in life's way,
    Clear, beautiful, and calm ;
And angels round it loved to stay,
    And sing their Eden psalm.
And flowers of sweetness round it bloomed ;
    And odorous plants of balm.

The gentlest breath,—the lightest sigh
    Would stir its depths so clear :
Each tone of love that whispered by
    An answering voice might hear.
The softest light might find a smile,—
    The faintest sigh a tear.

The meanest flower, the lowliest thing,
    Obtained her ready love.
The household robin, with his wing,
    Would her soft tresses move.
In drawing near to her, he seemed
    No nat'ral fears to prove.

She loved each lowly place serene
   Where humblest blossoms grew :
Each little spot of pleasant green
   Her sweet affections drew.
She loved God's earth—and loved the light.
   High in His heaven of blue.

The misty hills won not her heart,
   In distant, towering pride,
Until she viewed them as a part
   (All fair and sanctified)
Of God's creative love ; *His* work.
   Who on the cross hath died.

And when she listened to the gush
   Of their rejoicing springs,
And saw the tender sunshine flush
   The tempest's lurid wings,
Ah, *then*, the mountains were enrolled
   Amongst belovèd things.

Yet was she still the playful child,
    With limbs so round and free ;
And step all vigorous and wild ;
    And voice of frolic glee !
And heart brim-full of life's delight,
    And wild-wood ecstasy.

Hush ! 'Tis the same dear steps which fall
    With softest, gentlest tread,
Obedient to the faintest call
    Breathed from her mother's bed,
To hand the cup, the pillow smooth,
    Or soothe the aching head.

Hush ! 'Tis the same clear voice, though stilled
    Down to its lowest key,
When wakeful chords of love are thrilled
    By touch of sympathy.
Ah, then, how delicate their tone !
    How soft ! how silvery !

She was not ours. Lord! she was Thine,
    Who, for a gladdening while,
Didst lend that little lamp, to shine
    Irradiate with Thy smile:
Then placed it in Thy heavenly courts,
    Where nothing shall defile.

Though shadows lie across our way,
    E'er since her light hath fled,
The lamp still burns with holier ray,
    By oil of gladness fed.
She was not ours. She was His own,
    Who for her ransom bled.

And *thou* wert also His,— not ours.—
    Oh precious Second-born!
Thou sweetest of all fragrant flowers:
    Thou rose without a thorn!
Thou brightest dewdrop on the spray,
    In spring's most dewy morn!

A sparkling brook! yet oft unseen,
   As on it blithely welled,
But for a line of living green
   Which marked the course it held;
And but for tones—sweet tones that rose
   Where'er its ripple swelled.

The thirsting flowers bent down, to kiss
   The fertilizing wave;
Its chosen course,—its dearest bliss
   To gladden and to lave!
And pleasant, to each passer-by,
   The music which it gave!

Then He, who loved and watched its tide,
   (Himself the Fount of light)
Did send His Spirit down to guide
   Its lovely course aright;
To deepen its enriching wave,
   And stem it with His might.

Alas! we see that line no more,
    Of bright and living green;
Alas! the buds around its shore,
    Of late, athirst have been;
And the mild blessings of its course
    To pilgrim eyes unseen:

For God hath turned our brooklet back
    To Zion's fount of love;
And led it from its earthly track
    To urns of light above;
And Seraphs, in their hymns of praise,
    Her choral sweetness prove!

TO MARY.

Fifteen springs ago, sweet Mary,
    Came a heavy cloud of woe,
Dark with mystery, and very
    Blighting, seen from earth below;

Very bright and very glorious,
    Seen from Love's own home above;
Where the angels, in their chorus,
    Paused, as if in raptured love,

To roll back the pearly portal
    Of the heavenly domain,
And receive to bliss immortal —
    Suddenly — thy sisters twain!

Ah! Life's roselight and its golden
 Paled, and well-nigh vanished *then;*
And the springtide flowers unfolding,
 Ne'er have looked the same again.

Yet, amidst the blight and sadness,
 Blossomed on the drooping bough,
Soon, a gift of dewy gladness—
 And this Maytide gift wert *thou!*

Thus was little Mary reckoned
 'Mongst the stricken band on earth:
Mortals count her but the *second*
 Daughter,—*Angels* count her *fourth!*

Both be right!—To thee are given
 Duties of a twofold kind;
And the claims of earth and heaven
 Thus be softly intertwined.

Daughter of the loved and living!
    Sister of the saints in rest!
Daughter of the trusting, striving!
    Sister of the crowned and blest!

Daughter! be thou faithful-hearted
    To the loved, thus sore bereft!
Sister of the bright departed!
    Be thou brightener of the left.

Ever mindful of a *second*
    Daughter's genial place on earth;
Mindful, too, that thou art beckoned
    Heavenward, as the precious *fourth!*

MY GRANDMOTHER'S WALKING-CANE.

WITH reverent love I call to mind,
    And picture, o'er again,
The feeble hand which used to rest
    Upon that polished cane.
Things bright and fair dissolve in air,
    And strong wax weak — but ah!
I see *thee*, clear as yesterday,
    My long-lost Grandmamma!

The bonnet, and the silken cloak,
    With quaintly fashioned hood;
The plaiting of the cambric sleeve,
    Held by its golden stud;

The ample gown of poplin brown,
  With long and flowing train ;
And the mittened hand which leaned for strength
  Upon the Indian cane.

Alas! It was a halting step,
  It was a faltering pace ;
But there was love which faltered not
  Upon her gentle face.
And there was light, from out of sight,
  Upon that reverend head,
From regions whither she was bound,
  With firm and steady tread.

I mind me how my young round hand,
  Did love to clear away
The small fir-cones and pebble stones
  That in her pathway lay ;
Scarce wotting half the patient love
  That strove, with soft caress,

To sweep the thorns from off the path
   Of childhood motherless!

Alas! The step on gravelled walk
   Grew rare—and yet more rare;
And then—instead of staff and shoe,
   The slow-paced wheeling chair;
And then—ah me! they folded up
   The out-of-doors attire,
And placed the padded elbow chair
   Beside the chamber fire.

I mind me (how should I forget?)
   My footstool at her knee;
The quiet talk—the dainty cup
   From which she sipped her tea.
I mind me of the "bon-bon" box.
   The trinkets, quaint and old;
And Queen Penelope, embossed
   On watch of massive gold.

But, more than all, the patient smile—
    The meek and gentle voice—
The whispered "*Hush!*" which quickly checked
    The too hilarious noise—
The listening ear—the ready tear
    For others' grief or pain:—
But wherefore dive for memory's pearls
    Adown life's troubled main?

There was a sound of startled feet,
    Fast hurrying to and fro,
And then a hush of quietness,
    And movements dull and slow;
And then—ah, me! in darkened rooms
    Our tear-drops fell like rain;
And then they placed aside the chair,
    And put away the cane!

We knew that she was gone to dwell
    Amongst a shining throng,

Where He who was her staff and stay
   Is now her strength and song —
Where weakness is exchanged for might,
   And shadows fade in truth —
And death in life — and hoary age
   In everlasting youth!

HYMN.

"I will bless the Lord at all times."

Oh, Thou, whose bounty fills my cup
　With every blessing meet,
I give Thee thanks for *every drop*—
　The bitter and the sweet!

I praise Thee for the desert road,
　And for the river-side—
For all Thy goodness hath bestowed,
　And all Thy grace denied!—

I thank Thee both for smile and frown,
　And for the gain and loss;
I praise Thee for the future crown,
　And for the present cross!—

I thank Thee for the wing of love
   Which stirred my worldly nest,
And for the stormy cloud that drove
   The flutterer to Thy breast! —

I bless Thee for the glad increase,
   And for the waning joy;
And for this strange, this settled peace,
   Which nothing can destroy!

THE END.

London: Printed by G. BARCLAY, Castle St. Leicester Sq.

June 1859

Works Published

BY

HATCHARD AND CO.

187 PICCADLLY, LONDON, W.

BOSWELL, Rev. M.—Baptism, considered in its Nature and Effects. With an Appendix, containing an Explanation of those Passages of Holy Scripture which relate to the subject. By the Rev. MARTIN BOSWELL, M.A. formerly Fellow of Clare College, Cambridge. Fcap. cloth, 2s.

Bow in the Cloud: a Memoir of M. E. H. By her SISTER, Author of "Ellen Mordaunt." Fcap. cloth, 3s. 6d.

"A simple, but touching biography. It records the trials and the consolations of one whose father died after a lingering illness, shortly before the period of her own ..... tion; and whose mother survived the shock for a few months only. The experience of sorrow is thus sketched, under no ordinary circumstances, by the only surviving member of the family. There is nothing of maudlin sentimentalism in the book, it conveys weighty lessons to the Christian reader."—*Liverpool Courier.*

BRADLEY, Rev. A.—Sermons, chiefly on Character: preached at Hale, Surrey. By the Rev. ARTHUR BRADLEY, M.A. Perpetual Curate of Hale, and Michel Fellow of Queen's College, Oxford. Fcap. cloth, 5s.

BRADLEY, Rev. C.—Sermons, preached chiefly at the Celebration of the Lord's Supper. By the Rev. CHARLES BRADLEY, Vicar of Glasbury, Brecknockshire. Third Edition. 8vo. cloth, 10s. 6d.

—— Practical Sermons for every Sunday and Principal Holyday in the Year. Fourth Edition. Complete in 1 vol. 8vo. cloth, 12s.

—— Sermons preached in the Parish Church of Glasbury, Brecknockshire, and St. James's Chapel, Clapham, Surrey. Ninth Edition. In 1 vol. 8vo. cloth, 10s. 6d.

—— Sermons on some of the Trials, Duties, and Encouragements of the Christian Life. Second Edition. 8vo. cloth, 10s. 6d.

—— Sunday Questions for Families and the Junior Classes in Schools. 18mo. cloth, 1s.

BURTT, J.—Exempla Necessaria; or, Elementary Latin Exercises on all the Parts of Speech, and the Substance of Syntax; containing English Words and Sentences to be turned into Latin, Latin into English, and numerous Examination Questions to be entered on with the Accidence. With an Introduction. By J. BURTT, Teacher of Latin, &c. Third Edition, much enlarged. 18mo. cloth, 2s. 6d.

CANTERBURY, Archbishop of.—Practical Reflections on Select Passages of the New Testament. By JOHN BIRD SUMNER, D.D., Lord Archbishop of Canterbury. Chiefly compiled from Expository Lectures on the Gospels and Epistles, by the same Author. Post 8vo. cloth, 5s. 6d.

—— A Practical Exposition of the New Testament, in the form of Lectures, intended to assist the practice of Domestic Instruction and Devotion. 9 vols. 8vo. cloth (each volume being a separate work), price 9s. each.

—— Christian Charity; its Obligations and Objects, with reference to the present state of Society. In a series of Sermons. Second Edition. 8vo. cloth, 9s.; or 12mo. 6s.

—— Apostolical Preaching Considered, in an Examination of St. Paul's Epistles. Also, Four Sermons on Subjects relating to the Christian Ministry, and preached on different occasions. Ninth Edition, enlarged, 8vo. cloth, 10s. 6d.

—— The Evidences of Christianity, derived from its Nature and Reception. Seventh Edition, 8vo. cloth, 10s. 6d.; or fcap. 3s.

—— A Series of Sermons on the Christian Faith and Character. Eighth Edition, 8vo. cloth, 10s. 6d.; or 12mo. 6s.

—— A Treatise on the Records of the Creation, and on the Moral Attributes of the Creator. Sixth Edition, 8vo. cloth, 10s. 6d.

CHAMBERS, Miss A.—Comfort in Sleepless Nights. Passages selected by ANNE CHAMBERS. Royal 8vo. (large type) cloth, 5s. 6d.

Christ our Example. By the Author of "The Listener." Eighth Edition. Fcap. cloth, 5s.
Contents.—1. In the Object of Life—2. In the Rule of Life—3. In his Intercourse with the World—4. In the Condition of Life—5. In his Sorrows—6. In his Joys—7. In his Death.

Christian Observer, conducted by Members of the Established Church. Published monthly, price 1s. 6d.

Christian Sympathy; a Collection of Letters addressed to Mourners. 32mo. cloth, gilt edges, 2s. 6d.

CHURTON, Rev. H. B. W.—Thoughts on the Land of the Morning; a Record of Two Visits to Palestine, 1849-50. By H. B. WHITAKER CHURTON, M.A. Vicar of Icklesham, Sussex, Chaplain to the Lord Bishop of Chichester, and late Preacher of the Charterhouse. Second Edition, corrected and enlarged. Crown 8vo. with numerous Illustrations, cloth, 10s. 6d.

CLOSE, Dean.—Miscellaneous Sermons, preached at Cheltenham. By the Very Rev. F. CLOSE, D.D. Dean of Carlisle. Second Edition. 2 vols. 8vo. boards, 21s.

Common Sense for Housemaids. By A LADY. Third Edition, corrected. 12mo. 1s.

Companion to the Book of Common Prayer of the United Church of England and Ireland. 24mo. cloth, 2s. 6d.

Consistency. By CHARLOTTE ELIZABETH. Sixth Edition. 18mo. boards, 2s. 6d.

Constance and Edith; or, Incidents of Home Life. By a CLERGYMAN'S WIFE. Fcap. cloth, 4s. 6d.

"This is one of those simple quiet tales of English domestic life which afford pleasure to youthful readers; its tone is religious and moral, lessons being also conveyed on us, ful practical points in regard to behaviour and conduct. It is a tale that may be safely and with advantage put into the hands of children."—*Literary Gazette.*

"A well-intentioned and pleasant tale, really consisting of 'Incidents of Home Life.'"—*Spectator.*

"The story is sufficiently varied in its incidents to sustain the attention of the reader throughout."—*Morning Post.*

"This is a pleasing book for young people, and, as such, we are glad to recommend it."—*Church of England Magazine.*

"This interesting tale will become a great favourite with both parents and children."—*Morning Herald.*

COURTENAY, Bishop.—The Future States, their Evidences and Nature: considered on Principles Physical, Moral, and Scriptural, with the Design of showing the Value of Gospel Revelation. By the Right Rev. REGINALD COURTENAY, D.D. Lord Bishop of Kingston, Jamaica. 8vo. cloth, 6s.

COUTTS, Miss BURDETT.—A Summary Account of Prizes for Common Things, offered and awarded by Miss Burdett Coutts at the Whitelands Training Institution. Second Edition, greatly enlarged, 8vo. cloth, 1s. 6d.

CRUDEN, A.—A complete Concordance to the Holy Scriptures of the Old and New Testament; or, A Dictionary and Alphabetical Index to the Bible. In Two Parts. To which is added, A Concordance to the Apocrypha. By ALEXANDER CRUDEN, M.A. The Ninth Edition. With a Life of the Author, by ALEXANDER CHALMERS, F.S.A. 4to. boards, 1l. 1s.

CUNNINGHAM, Rev. J. W.—Sermons. By the Rev. J. W. CUNNINGHAM, A.M. Vicar of Harrow, and late Fellow of St. John's College, Cambridge. Fifth Edition. 2 vols. 8vo. bds. 1l. 1s.

——— Six Lectures on the Book of Jonah. Fcap. boards, 3s.

——— The Velvet Cushion. Eleventh Edition. Fcap. boards, 5s.

DRUMMOND, H.—Social Duties on Christian Principles. By HENRY DRUMMOND, Esq. M.P. Fifth Edition. Fcap. cloth, 4s.

EDELMAN, Rev. W.—Sermons on the History of Joseph. Preached in the Parish Church of St. Mary, Wimbledon. By the Rev. W. EDELMAN, Perpetual Curate of Merton. 12mo. cloth, 5s.

——— The Family Pastor; or, Short Sermons for Family Reading. 12mo. cloth, 3s. 6d.

EDMUNDS, Rev. J.—The Seven Sayings of Christ on the Cross. Seven Lent Lectures. To which is prefixed, a Gospel Harmony of the Passion of our Lord and Saviour Jesus Christ. With Explanatory Notes. By the Rev. JOHN EDMUNDS, M.A. formerly Fellow of the University of Durham. Fcap. cloth, 3s. 6d.

——— Sermons, preached for the most part in a Country Church in the Diocese of Durham. Second Series. Fcap. cloth, 5s. 6d.

"The Sermons contained in this volume are generally sound and eminently practical, and admirably adapted for the purpose for which they are published—to be read in families to children and servants on the Sunday evening."—*John Bull.*

Eighteen Maxims of Neatness and Order. To which is prefixed an Introduction by THERESA TIDY. Twenty-fourth Edition. 18mo. sewed, 6d.

ELLIOTT, Rev. C. B.—The Rev. C. B. Elliott's Horæ
Apocalypticæ; Abridged for the School-room, and for Family Reading. Second Edition, revised and corrected. With a Recommendatory Notice by the Author of the " Horæ Apocalypticæ." Fcap. cloth, 5s.

Ethel Woodville; or, Woman's Ministry. A Tale for the Times. 2 vols. fcap. cloth, 12s.

" ' Ethel Woodville' is a tale told by a graceful and a pious pen. Its moral is, that no woman can expect happiness if she be united to a man not having the fear of God. The character of the heroine is finely and tenderly drawn, and the whole progress of the story moves gracefully and gently. There is no turmoil, no exciting scenes ; and yet it may be read without weariness, but certainly not without profit."—THE CRITIC.

"A clever story: we can recommend it as being considerably above the common level of its kind."—LITERARY GAZETTE.

Far off: Part I.; or Asia Described. With Anecdotes and numerous Illustrations. By the Author of "Peep of Day,". &c. Sixteenth Thousand. Fcap. cloth, 4s.

" We have sometimes met clergymen who are in the habit of endeavouring to promote the Missionary cause in their parishes, who would be thankful for such a little book as this. It seems to us just the sort of book that might be read out to a class of young persons, either in National Schools or otherwise, and which would be certain to interest them exceedingly."—*English Review.*

—— Part II.; or, Africa and America Described.
With Anecdotes and numerous Illustrations. Tenth Thousand. Fcap. cloth, 4s.

FENELON.—Extracts from the Religious Works of
Fenelon, Archbishop of Cambray. Translated from the Original French by Miss MARSHALL. Eleventh Edition, with a Portrait. Fcap. cloth, 5s.

FINCHER, J.—The Achievements of Prayer.
Selected exclusively from the Holy Scriptures. By the late JOSEPH FINCHER, Esq. With a Testimony to the Work by the late James Montgomery. Third Edition. 12mo. cloth, 6s.

FORSYTH, Rev. J. H.—Sermons by the late Rev.
JOHN HAMILTON FORSYTH, M.A. Curate of Weston-super-Mare, and afterwards Minister of Dowry Chapel, Clifton, Domestic Chaplain to the Marquis of Thomond. With a Memoir of the Author, by the Rev. EDWARD WILSON, M.A. Vicar of Nocton, Lincolnshire. Third Edition. 8vo. cloth, with Portrait, 10s. 6d.

"The character of Mr. Forsyth is one which we greatly admire," &c.— *Christian Observer.*

GARBETT, Archdeacon.—Christ on Earth, in Heaven, and on the Judgment-seat. By the Ven. JAMES GARBETT, M.A. Archdeacon of Chichester. 2 vols. 12mo. cloth, 12s.

"No one can read these volumes without great delight and profit."—*Christian Observer.*

—— Parochial Sermons. 2 vols. 8vo. cloth, each 12s.

—— Christ as Prophet, Priest, and King; being a Vindication of the Church of England from Theological Novelties. In Eight Lectures, preached before the University of Oxford, at Canon Bampton's Lecture, 1842. 2 vols. 8vo. cloth 1l. 4s.

—— The Beatitudes of the Mount. In Seventeen Sermons. 12mo. cloth, 7s.

"There is a depth and a solidity in these discourses, which favourably distinguish them from so many of the superficial productions with which the press is teeming. The reader cannot but feel that he has something worth thinking of presented to him; and the more he ponders them the greater will be his profit."—*Church of England Magazine.*

GIBBON, E.—The History of the Decline and Fall of the Roman Empire. By EDWARD GIBBON, Esq. New Edition. 8 vols. 8vo. cloth, 3l.

GIBSON, Bishop.—The Sacrament of the Lord's Supper Explained; or, the Things to be known and done to make a worthy Communicant. With suitable Prayers and Meditations. By EDMUND GIBSON, D.D. late Lord Bishop of London. New Edition, Fcap. cloth, 2s. 6d.

—— Family Devotion; or, an Exhortation to Morning and Evening Prayer in Families; with two Forms of Prayer, suited to those two Seasons, and also fitted for the use of one Person in Private, &c. (Reprinted from the Eighteenth Edition.) Fcap. cloth, 2s.

The Gipsies. Dedicated, by permission, to JAMES CRABB, the Gipsies' Friend. Fcap. cloth, 4s. 6d.

GOODE, Rev. F.—The Better Covenant practically Considered, from Heb. viii. 6, 10-12; with a Supplement on Philip. ii. 12, 13, and Notes. By the late Rev. F. GOODE, M.A. Fifth Edition. To which is added, A Sermon on Jer. xxxi. 31-34. Fcap. cloth, 7s.

A 2

GOODE, Rev. W.—The Nature of Christ's Presence in the Eucharist; or, the True Doctrine of the Real Presence Vindicated; in opposition to the fictitious Real Presence asserted by Archdeacon Denison, Mr. (late Archdeacon) Wilberforce, and Dr. Pusey; with full proof of the real character of the attempt made by those authors to represent their doctrine as that of the Church of England and her divines. By WILLIAM GOODE, M.A. F.S.A. Rector of St. Margaret, Lothbury. 2 vols. 8vo. cloth, 24s.

—— Aid for Determining some Disputed Points in the Ceremonial of the Church of England. Second Edition, 8vo. cloth, 4s.

—— A Vindication of the Doctrine of the Church of England on the Validity of the Orders of the Scotch and Foreign Non-Episcopal Churches. 8vo. cloth, 5s.

—— The Doctrine of the Church of England as to the Effects of Baptism in the case of Infants. With an Appendix, containing the Baptismal Services of Luther and the Nuremberg and Cologne Liturgies. Second Edition. 8vo. cloth, 15s.

The Gospel of Other Days; or, Thoughts on Old and New Testament Scriptures. By the Author of "Seed Time and Harvest." 18mo. cloth, 2s.

"We heartily welcome the little book . . . . As a sound and eminently practical compression of a great subject into a very small compass, we can heartily recommend it."—*Bickersteth's Weekly Visitor.*

GRAGLIA, C.—A Pocket Dictionary of the Italian and English Languages. By C. GRAGLIA. Square 18mo. bound, 4s. 6d.

GRAY, Mrs. H.—History of Rome for Young Persons. With numerous Wood Engravings. Second Edition, corrected. By Mrs. HAMILTON GRAY. 1 vol. 12mo. cloth, 8s.

"A very ingenious attempt to bring the recent discoveries of the critical school into working competition with the miserable Goldsmiths and Pinnocks of our youth."—*Christian Remembrancer.*

"The clear, lively, and pleasing style of narration is admirably calculated to awaken and sustain the attention."—*Athenæum.*

—— Emperors of Rome from Augustus to Constantine: being a Continuation of the History of Rome. 1 vol. 12mo. with Illustrations, 8s.

"So many applications are made to us for histories suited to a period of life when the mind is beginning to develope its power, and to find satisfaction in connecting the past with the present and the future in human affairs, that we are induced to recommend these volumes, which, however widely circulated, have not half the circulation which they deserve. They are clearly written. They neither minister to childish im-

GRAY, Mrs. H.

bocility, nor take for granted a measure of knowledge which cannot be lawfully expected of the young. They present the page of history as it really is—not a series of dry details, nor of gorgeous spectacles, but with enough of plain fact to instruct the understanding, and of romantic incident to kindle the sympathies and affections."—*Christian Observer.*

"We have no hesitation in saying, that this is one of the best histories of the Roman Empire for children and young people which has come under our notice. Mrs. Hamilton Gray has made herself acquainted with at least some of the more important ancient writers on the subject of which she treats, and also with the criticisms of Niebuhr and other modern investigators of Roman history."—*Athenæum.*

"It may be recommended as a clear, rapid, and well-arranged summary of facts, pointed by frequent but brief reflections. . . . The book is a very good compendium of the Imperial History, primarily designed for children, but useful for all."—*Spectator.*

"It would be an erroneous impression to convey of this volume, that it is written solely for schools and children. In reality it is an abridgment far more likely to be useful to grown-up persons, who can reflect upon the working of general laws, and make their own observations upon men and things. A striking characteristic of the book is the impartiality of its political tone, and its high moral feeling."—*Examiner.*

—— The History of Etruria. Part I. Tarchun and his Times. From the Foundation of Tarquinia to the Foundation of Rome. Part II. From the Foundation of Rome to the General Peace of Anno Tarquiniensis, 839, B.C. 348. 2 vols. post 8vo. cloth, each 12s.

"A work which we strongly recommend as certain to afford pleasure and profit to every reader."—*Athenæum.*

—— Tour to the Sepulchres of Etruria in 1839. Third Edition. With numerous Illustrations, post 8vo. cloth, 1l. 1s.

"Mrs. Gray has won an honourable place in the large assembly of modern female writers."—*Quarterly Review.*

"We warmly recommend Mrs. Gray's most useful and interesting volume."—*Edinburgh Review.*

GRAY, Miss A. T.—The Twin Pupils; or, Education at Home. A Tale addressed to the Young. By ANN THOMSON GRAY. Fcap. cloth, 7s. 6d.

"The story is well planned, well varied, and well written."—*Spectator.*

"More sound principles and useful practical remarks we have not lately met in any work on the much-treated subject of education. The book is written with liveliness as well as good sense."—*Literary Gazette.*

"A volume of excellent tendency, which may be put with safety and advantage into the hands of well-educated young people."—*Evangelical Magazine.*

GRIFFITH, Rev. T.—The Spiritual Life. By the Rev. THOMAS GRIFFITH, A.M. Minister of Ram's Episcopal Chapel, Homerton. Eighth Edition. Fcap. cloth, 4s.

—— Sermons preached in St. James's Chapel, Ryde. Second Edition. Fcap. cloth, 5s.

—— Live while you Live. Seventh Edition. 18mo. cloth, 1s. 6d.

GRIFFITH, Rev. T.

—— The Lord's Prayer: contemplated as the Expression of the Primary Elements of Devoutness. Second Edition. Fcap. cloth, 2s.

—— The Lord's Supper: its Nature, Requirements, Benefits. Third Edition. Fcap. cloth, 1s. 6d.

—— Confirmation, and the Baptismal Vow for Catechumens, Communicants, Parents, and Sponsors; with Practical Helps for Catechumens. Fourth Edition. Fcap. cloth, 2s.

—— Confirmation: its Object, Importance, and Benefit; with Practical Helps for those about to be Confirmed. Sixth Edition. Price 4d. or 3s. 6d. per doz.

—— Our Baptismal Standing Practically Considered. 12mo. price 6d.

GRIMSTON, Hon. Miss.—Arrangement of the Common Prayer-Book and Lessons. Dedicated, by Permission, to Her Majesty.

The peculiar advantage of this arrangement consists in having the entire Morning and Evening Services printed in a clear type, in two portable volumes, one for the Morning and the other for the Evening.

	£	s.	d.
Royal 32mo. morocco, elegant	1	4	0
Ditto plain	1	1	0
Ditto calf, gilt leaves	0	16	0

HANKINSON, Rev. T. E.— Poems. By THOMAS EDWARDS HANKINSON, M.A. late of Corpus Christi College, Cambridge, and Minister of St. Matthew's Chapel, Denmark Hill. Edited by his Brothers. Fourth Edition. Fcap. cloth, 7s.

—— Sermons. 8vo. cloth, 10s. 6d.

HARE, Rev. A. W.—Sermons to a Country Congregation. By AUGUSTUS WILLIAM HARE, A.M. late Fellow of New College, and Rector of Alton Barnes. Eighth Edition. 2 vols. 12mo. cloth, 14s.

"They are, in truth, as appears to us, compositions of very rare merit, and realise a notion we have always entertained, that a sermon for our rural congregations there somewhere was, if it could be hit off, which in language should be familiar without being plain, and in matter solid without being abstruse."—*Quarterly Review.*

HASTINGS, Rev. H. J.—Parochial Sermons, from Trinity to Advent. By HENRY JAMES HASTINGS, M.A. Honorary Canon of Worcester, Rural Dean, Rector of Martley, Worcestershire. 8vo. cloth, 12s.

HATCHARD, Rev. T. G.—The Floweret Gathered; a Brief Memoir of a Departed Daughter. By T. GOODWIN HATCHARD, M.A. Rector of St. Nicholas, Guildford. Third Thousand. Square 16mo. 1s.

"This is an account of one of the lambs of Christ's fold, who exhibited the truest simplicity and natural character of a child, united to unwavering trust in and love to that Saviour, who took her early to himself. It is calculated both to interest, and, we trust, greatly to profit, our young friends, as a pattern of early piety."—*Church of England Sunday-school Monthly Magazine for Teachers.*

"No one can rise from the perusal of this little volume without feeling deeply interested in the lovely character of the dear Addie."—*Jewish Intelligence.*

"This is a touching little narrative for the young. Few will read it without a full heart, and the shedding of a tear of sweet sympathy with 'The Floweret Gathered.'"—*Children's Jewish Advocate.*

—— Thanksgiving; or, The Wave-Offering and the Heave-Offering. A Harvest Sermon preached in Havant Church on Sunday, August 20, 1854. 8vo. price 6d.

—— The German Tree; or, a Moral for the Young. Price 1s.

—— Feed My Lambs: a Lecture for Children in Words of One Syllable; to which is added a Hymn. Seventh Thousand. 32mo. 3d.; or 2s. 6d. per dozen.

—— Food for my Flock: being Sermons delivered in the Parish Church of Havant, Hants. Fcap. cloth, 5s. 6d.

"These Sermons are marked by unaffected piety, great clearness of exposition, and a direct plainness of style and purpose which render them pre-eminently practical."—*Britannia.*

"A set of plain, spirited discourses, which are not unlikely to disturb the repose of the drowsy, and to send home simple truths to the hearts that heed them. The Sermons are, besides, scriptural in their doctrinal views, charitable in temper, unpolemical, rather asserting the truth than contending for it."—*Christian Observer.*

HATHERELL, Rev. Dr.—The Signs of the Second Advent of our Blessed Lord, collected from the words of Jesus and applied to our own times. In Twelve Sermons, preached during the season of Advent, in the years 1856 and 1857, in the Church of St. James, West-end, Southampton. By JAMES WILLIAMS HATHERELL, D.D. Incumbent. 12mo. cloth, 5s.

14　　　　　*Works Published by*

HEPPE, Dr.—The Reformers of England and Germany in the Sixteenth Century; their Intercourse and Correspondence. A Historical Sketch, including valuable Original Documents. By Dr. HEPPE, of Marburg, Author of "A History of Protestantism," &c. Translated, with additions, including hitherto unpublished letters from Martin Luther and Justus Jonas to Thomas Cromwell. By the Rev. Hermann Schmettau and Rev. B. Harris Cowper. Fcap. cloth, 2s. 6d.

' This is a well-informed and beautiful volume, presenting a valuable selection of historic facts touching great men, the instruments of producing a great revolution in human affairs."—BRITISH BANNER.

HEY, Mrs.—The Holy Places, a series of Sonnets; and other Poems. By REBECCA HEY, Author of "The Moral of Flowers," "The Spirit of the Woods," "Recollections of the Lakes," &c. &c. Fcap. cloth, 5s.

"'The Holy Places and other Poems' are of no common order: the thoughts being finely conceived, and the expression very perfect. The Sonnets deserve to be generally known."—CLERICAL JOURNAL.

"Chaste, sweet, and musical are these poems. There is a spirit of natural poetry in every throb of her muse, and one can hardly rise from a perusal of this little volume without having imbibed pleasure and instruction."—CRITIC.

"There is vigour and freshness about these poems, combined with much real earnestness of purpose."—BELL'S MESSENGER.

"These poems are conceived in an eminently pious spirit, and marked by a very fair amount of literary ability. The proceeds of the work are to be devoted to the aid of the Special Missions in India."—THE STAR.

Hints on Early Education and Nursery Discipline.
Sixteenth Edition. 12mo. cloth, 3s. 6d.

Hints for Reflection. Compiled from various Authors.
Third Edition. 32mo. cloth, 2s.

HODGSON, Rev. C.—Family Prayers for One Month. By various Clergymen. Arranged and Edited by the Rev. CHARLES HODGSON, M.A. Rector of Barton-le-Street, Yorkshire. Abridged Edition. To which have been added, Prayers for Particular Seasons.

Amongst the Contributors are His Grace the Archbishop of Canterbury, the late Rev. Chancellor Raikes, the Ven. Archdeacon Sandford, the late Rev. J. Haldane Stewart, Rev. Charles Bridges, Rev. C. A. Thurlow, the late Rev. E. Bickersteth, &c. &c. Fcap. cloth, 3s. 6d.

Holidays at Lynmere; or, Conversations on the Miracles of our Lord.
By a LADY. Edited by the Rev. CHARLES F. MACKENZIE, M.A. Fellow of Caius College, Cambridge. 18mo. cloth, 3s. 6d.

Hatchard and Co. 187 *Piccadilly.* 15

HOPE, Dr.—Memoirs of the late James Hope, M.D. Physician to St. George's Hospital, &c. &c. By Mrs. HOPE. To which are added, Remarks on Classical Education, by Dr. HOPE. And Letters from a Senior to a Junior Physician, by Dr. BURDER. The whole edited by KLEIN GRANT, M.D. &c. &c. Fourth Edition. Post 8vo. cloth, 7s.

"The general, as well as the medical reader, will find this a most interesting and instructive volume."—*Gentleman's Magazine.*
"A very interesting memoir to every class of readers."—*Christian Observer.*

HUME and SMOLLETT.—The History of England, from the Invasion of Julius Cæsar to the Death of George the Second. By D. HUME and T. SMOLLETT. 10 vols. 8vo. cloth, 4*l*.

The Interrogator; or, Universal Ancient History, in Questions and Answers. By a LADY. 12mo. roan, 5s.

JACKSON, Rev. F.—Sermons. By the Rev. FREDERIC JACKSON, Incumbent of Parson Drove, Isle of Ely. 2 vols. fcap. cloth, each 5s.

"Discourses addressed to a village congregation. The chief aim of the preacher has been to enforce practical conclusions for the guidance of the humblest, from some of the most striking events or sentiments of Scripture. The style is plain and forcible."—*Spectator.*

JEWSBURY, Miss M. J.—Letters to the Young. By MARIA JANE JEWSBURY. Fifth Edition. Fcap. cloth, 5s.

Light in the Dwelling; or, a Harmony of the Four Gospels, with very Short and Simple Remarks adapted to Reading at Family Prayers, and arranged in 365 sections, for every day of the year. By the Author of "The Peep of Day," "Line upon Line," &c. Revised and Corrected by a Clergyman of the Church of England. Sixteenth Thousand. Post 8vo. cloth, 8s.; or in 8vo. large type, 10s.

Line upon Line; or, a Second Series of the Earliest Religious Instruction the Infant Mind is capable of receiving; with Verses illustrative of the Subjects. By the Author of "The Peep of Day," &c. Part I. Seventy-seventh Thousand. Part II. Sixty-seventh Thousand. 18mo. cloth, each 2*s*. 6*d*.

LITTON, Rev. E. A. — The Mosaic Dispensation considered as Introductory to Christianity. Eight Sermons preached before the University of Oxford, at the Bampton Lecture for 1856. By the Rev. EDWARD ARTHUR LITTON, M.A., late Fellow of Oriel College. 8vo. cloth, 10*s*. 6*d*.

"We most earnestly direct the deep and serious attention of undergraduates at our universities, and theological students generally, to these weighty and important lectures."—*Record.*

M'NEILE, Rev. Dr.—Lectures on the Sympathies, Sufferings, and Resurrection of the Lord Jesus Christ, delivered in Liverpool during Passion Week and Easter Day. By HUGH M'NEILE, D.D., Hon. Canon of Chester, and Incumbent of St. Paul's Church, Prince's Park, Liverpool. Third Edition. 12mo. cloth, 4s. 6d.

MARRIOTT, Rev. H.—Sermons on the Character and Duties of Women. By the Rev. HARVEY MARRIOTT, Vicar of Loddiswell, and Chaplain to the Right Honourable Lord Kenyon. 12mo. cloth, 3s. 6d.

—— Four Courses of Practical Sermons. 8vo. each 10s. 6d.

MARSDEN, Rev. J. B.—The History of the Early Puritans; from the Reformation to the Opening of the Civil War in 1642. By J. B. MARSDEN, M.A. Second Edition. 8vo. cloth, 10s. 6d.

—— The History of the later Puritans; from the Opening of the Civil War in 1642, to the Ejection of the Non-conforming Clergy in 1662. Second Edition. 8vo. cloth, 10s. 6d.

MARSHALL, Miss.—Extracts from the Religious Works of Fénélon, Archbishop of Cambray. Translated from the Original French by Miss MARSHALL. Eleventh Edition, with a Portrait. Fcap. cloth, 5s.

MEEK, Rev. R.—The Mutual Recognition and Exalted Felicity of Glorified Saints. By the Rev. ROBERT MEEK, M.A. Rector of St. Michael, Sutton Bonnington, Notts. Sixth Edition. Fcap. cloth, 3s. 6d.

—— Passion Week; a Practical and Devotional Exposition of the Gospels and Epistles appointed for that Season, composed for the Closet and the Family. 12mo. boards, 4s.

MEREWEATHER, Rev. J. D.—Diary of a Working Clergyman in Australia and Tasmania, kept during the years 1850-1853; including his Return to England by way of Java, Singapore, Ceylon, and Egypt. By the Rev. JOHN DAVIES MEREWEATHER, B.A. Author of "Life on Board an Emigrant Ship." Fcap. cloth, 5s.

"We set great store by this volume, which abounds in interesting facts touching men and things, times and places, strange people and savage manners."—BRITISH BANNER.

"There is an unassuming spirit of religious faith and devotion to his Master's cause, which speaks well for the practical Christianity of the author; and so varied and amusing are the scenes and characters he discusses, that, blended with felicitous and original observations upon both, the combination results in one of the most attractive books of the present season."—JOHN BULL.

MERRY, W.—Futurity. By WILLIAM MERRY,
Esq. Sixth Edition. Fcap. cloth, 2s.

"This is an excellent, nay, a beautiful little work. We recommend it to the perusal of doubters, and the enjoyment of believers—Christianity in its most affecting form to unsophisticated and rightly constituted minds."—TIMES.

"He has written on a pleasing subject, and written well; and it is impossible to read his little book without being the better for it. What is here advanced will assist the reader in the very important work of setting his affections on the things above. The nature of a future state of happiness, and its probable occupations, are treated in a pious and thoughtful manner."—CLERICAL JOURNAL.

Mid-Day Thoughts for the Weary. 32mo. cloth, 2s.

More about Jesus; a Sequel to "Peep of Day."
By the same Author. Eleventh Thousand. 18mo. cloth, with Illustrations by Harvey, 2s. 6d.

Near Home; or, the Countries of Europe described to Children, with Anecdotes. By the Author of "Peep of Day," "Light in the Dwelling," &c. Illustrated with numerous Wood Engravings. Twenty-eighth Thousand. Fcap. cloth, 5s.

"It must be very interesting to children. Those to whom we have read passages, taken at random, clap their little hands with delight."—*English Journal of Education.*

"A well-arranged and well-written book for children; compiled from the best writers on the various countries, and full of sound and useful information, pleasantly conveyed for the most part in the homely monosyllabic Saxon which children learn from their mothers and nurses."—*Athenæum.*

New Manual of Devotions; containing Family and Private Prayers, the Office for the Holy Communion, &c. 12mo. bd. 4s.

NEWNHAM, W.—A Tribute of Sympathy Addressed to Mourners. By W. NEWNHAM, Esq. Eleventh Edition. Fcap. cloth, 5s.

Contents:—1. Indulgence of Grief.—2. Moderation of Grief.—3. Excessive Sorrow.—4. Advantages of Sorrow.—5. Self-examination.—6. Resignation.—7. Sources of Consolation.

Night of Toil; or, a Familiar Account of the Labours of the First Missionaries in the South Sea Islands. By the Author of "The Peep of Day," "Near Home," &c. Fourth Edition. Fcap. cloth, 4s.

NIND, Rev. W.—Lecture-Sermons, preached in a Country Parish Church. By WILLIAM NIND, M.A. late Fellow of St. Peter's College, Cambridge, and Vicar of Cherry Hinton. Second Series. 12mo. cloth, 6s.

"Sermons distinguished by brevity, good sense, and a plainness of manner and exposition which well adapt them for family perusal, especially as their style is neat and simple, not bare."—*Spectator.*

"The many who have read the first volume of these sermons will welcome, no doubt with joy, the appearance of the second. They are readable and preachable; and those of the second volume are even plainer and simpler than their predecessors. We recommend both volumes most heartily."—*English Review.*

NORTHESK, Countess of.—The Sheltering Vine. Selections by the COUNTESS OF NORTHESK. With an Introduction by the Very Rev. R. C. TRENCH, D.D., Dean of Westminster. Sixth Thousand. 2 vols. small 8vo. cloth, 10s.

The object of this Work is to afford consolation under the various trials of mind and body to which all are exposed, by a Selection of Texts and Passages from Holy Scripture, and Extracts from Old and Modern Authors, in Prose and Poetry, with a Selection of Prayers adapted to the same.

—— A Selection of Prayers and Hymns, for the Use of her Children. In Two Parts, 12mo. sewed, 1s.; cloth, 2s.

NUGENT'S Pocket Dictionary of the French and English Languages. The Twenty-sixth Edition, revised by J. C. TARVER, French Master, Eton, &c. Square 18mo. bound, 4s. 6d.

OAKLEY, Rev. C. E.—The English Bible, and its History. A Lecture delivered in the School-room at Tortworth Court, Gloucestershire, January 23, 1854. By the Rev. C. E. OAKLEY, B.A. Rector of Wickwar, Gloucestershire, and Domestic Chaplain to the Earl of Ducie. Fcap. cloth, 1s. 6d.

OXENDEN, Rev. A.—The Cottage Library. Vol. I. The Sacrament of Baptism. By the Rev. ASHTON OXENDEN, Rector of Pluckley, Kent. 18mo. sewed, 1s.; or cloth, 1s. 6d.

"A little book of probably large usefulness. It avoids disputed points, but conveys a clear and simple view of the holy rite of baptism. It is admirably suited to the cottage, as well as to all places in which ignorance reigns upon the subject."—*Church and State Gazette.*

—— The Cottage Library. Vol. II. The Sacrament of the Lord's Supper. Third Edition. 18mo. cloth, 1s.

—— The Cottage Library. Vol. III. A Plain History of the Christian Church. Second Edition. 18mo. cloth, 1s.

OXENDEN, Rev. A.
—— The Cottage Library. Vol. IV. Fervent Prayer. 18mo.

—— The Cottage Library. Vol. V. God's Message to the Poor: being Eleven Plain Sermons preached in Pluckley Church. Second Edition. 18mo. cloth, 2s.

—— The Cottage Library. Vol. VI. The Story of Ruth. 18mo. cloth, 2s.

OXFORD, Bishop of.—Four Sermons, preached before Her Most Gracious Majesty Queen Victoria in 1841 and 1842. By SAMUEL, Lord Bishop of Oxford, Chancellor of the Most Noble Order of the Garter, Lord High Almoner to the Queen. Published by Command. Third Edition. Fcap. 8vo. cloth, 4s.

PARKER, Miss F. S.—Truth without Novelty; or, a Course of Scriptural Instruction for every Sunday in the Year, principally designed for Private Family Instruction and Sunday Schools. By FRANCES S. PARKER. Second Edition. Fcap. cloth, 3s.

PARRY, Sir W. E.—Thoughts on the Parental Character of God. By Rear-Admiral Sir WILLIAM EDWARD PARRY, R.N. late Lieut.-Governor of Greenwich Hospital. Fifth Edition. 18mo. cloth, 1s. 6d.

PEARS, Rev. S. A.—Over the Sea; or, Letters from an Officer in India to his Children at Home. Edited by the Rev. S. A. PEARS, D.D. Head-Master of Repton School. Fcap. cloth, with Illustrations. 4s. 6d.

"These letters from 'Over the Sea' contain just the kind of information that one wishes to have about the country and the people of India, and the mode of life of the English in the East. The description of scenery and sketches of native character and customs are graphic and entertaining, and the pictures are all the more vivid from the style being such as was deemed most adapted for youthful readers."—*Literary Gazette.*

"... their tone is so manly, sensible, and affectionate, with a pervading element of unobtrusive religious principle, that it is impossible to read them without a feeling of regard for the anonymous writer, and interest in his youthful correspondents."—*Guardian.*

"These letters possess two valuable qualities—reality and simplicity."—*Record.*

—— Three Lectures on Education. 18mo. cloth, 1s.

"The position occupied by Dr. Pears ought to give authority to his remarks on Education, and all that is contained in this little book is characterised by practical wisdom."—CLERICAL JOURNAL.

"We recommend this little book to the notice of every teacher and head of a family."—THE BEACON.

PEARSON, Rev. J. N.—Sunday Readings for the Family and the Closet. By the Rev. J. NORMAN PEARSON, M.A. 12mo. cloth, 7s.

"Sound and practical."—*British Magazine.*
"A most valuable work."—*Church of England Magazine.*

—— The Days in Paradise, in Six Lectures. 12mo. cloth, 3s.

Peep of Day; or, a Series of the Earliest Religious Instruction the Infant Mind is capable of receiving. With Verses illustrative of the Subjects. Hundred and Twenty-sixth Thousand, revised and corrected. 18mo. cloth, 2s.

—— Part II.; or, More about Jesus. By the same Author. Eleventh Thousand. 18mo. cloth, 2s. 6d.

Practical Suggestions towards Alleviating the Sufferings of the Sick. Part II. Fourth Edition. 12mo. cloth, 6s. 6d.

PRATT, Archdeacon.—Scripture and Science not at Variance: with Remarks on the Historical Character, Plenary Inspiration, and Surpassing Importance, of the Earlier Chapters of Genesis. By JOHN H. PRATT, M.A., Archdeacon of Calcutta; Author of the "Mathematical Principles of Mechanical Philosophy." Third Edition, with Additions, 8vo. cloth, 3s. 6d.

PRAYERS, Family and Private.

A Form of Prayers, Selected and Composed for the Use of a Family principally consisting of Young Persons. Thirteenth Edition. 12mo. cloth, 2s. 6d.

A Manual of Family and Occasional Prayers. By the Rev. WILLIAM SINCLAIR, M.A. 18mo. cloth, 1s. 6d.

A Selection of Prayers and Hymns. For the Use of her Children. By the COUNTESS OF NORTHESK. In Two Parts, 12mo. 2s. cloth; or sewed, 1s.

Family Prayers. By the late HENRY THORNTON, Esq. M.P. Thirty-sixth Edition. 12mo. cloth, 3s.

PRAYERS, Family and Private.

> **Family Prayers for One Month.** By various Clergymen. Arranged and Edited by the Rev. CHARLES HODGSON, M.A. Rector of Barton-le-Street, Yorkshire. Abridged Edition. To which have been added, Prayers for Particular Seasons. Fcap. cloth, 3s. 6d.

> **Seventy Prayers on Scriptural Subjects:** being a Selection of Scripture Daily Readings for a Year; with Family Prayers for a Month. By Clergymen of the Church of England. Fifth Ten Thousand. 12mo. cloth, 2s.

> **Family Prayers.** By the late W. WILBERFORCE, Esq. Edited by his Son. Eleventh Edition. Fcap. 8vo. sewed, 1s. 6d.

> **Family Prayers for Every Day of the Week.** Selected from various portions of the Holy Bible, with References. Third Edition. 12mo. boards, 2s. 6d.

> **Family Prayers for Every Day in the Week.** By CLERICUS. 18mo. cloth, 1s. 6d.

> **Prayers and Offices of Devotion for Families** and for Particular Persons, upon most occasions. By BENJAMIN JENKS. Altered and Improved by the Rev. CHARLES SIMEON. 12mo. roan, 4s. 6d.; or 18mo. 3s.

> **Short Family Prayers for Every Morning and** Evening of the Month. Selected and Arranged from the Liturgy, Psalms, and various eminent Writers. By WILLIAM SOLTAU, Esq. Member of the Church of England. Second Edition. 12mo. cloth, 3s.

> **A Course of Morning and Evening Prayers, for** the Use of the Families of the Poor. 12mo. sewed, 6d.; or 5s. per dozen.

> **Private Prayers for Young Persons.** By M. A. Fcap. cloth, 2s.

PRAYERS, Family and Private.

A Few Plain Short Prayers, intended to be sent with each set of Baby Linen lent to Poor Women. 24mo. sewed, 3d.; or 2s. 6d. per dozen.

A Companion to the Altar, with Occasional Prayers. By GEORGE A. E. MARSH, A.M. Rector of Bangor, Flintshire. Third Edition. Boards, 1s. 6d.; sheep, 2s.; calf, 3s.

Newly-Arranged Manual for Communicants at the Lord's Supper, including the Service for the Holy Communion. 24mo. bound, 3s.

Prussian Oculist. A Manual of Information respecting the Ober Medicinal Rath de Leuw of Gräfrath. By An ENGLISH CLERGYMAN. Second Edition, 18mo. cloth, 2s.

RAIKES, Rev. H.—Sermons and Essays. By the Rev. HENRY RAIKES, late Chancellor of the Diocese of Chester. 8vo. cloth, 9s.

"It is needless to say that everything in the volume bears the impress of the author's mind and character. Sound evangelical doctrine is exhibited in elegant language, and illustrated from the resources of a cultivated understanding and a refined taste; while the whole is pervaded with Christian toleration and sound good sense."—*Evangelical Christendom.*

RAWNSLEY, Rev. R. D. B.—Sermons Preached in Country Churches. By R. DRUMMOND B. RAWNSLEY, M.A. Vicar of Shiplake, Oxon; late Fellow of Magdalen College, Oxford. 12mo. cloth, 6s.

"A series of short, plain, and pithy sermons, adapted to the character and comprehension of a rural congregation."—*Spectator.*
"A good volume; we can safely recommend it."—*St. James's Chronicle.*

—— Village Sermons. Second Series. 12mo. 5s. 6d.

"Enforces the practical duties of religion and the beauty of holiness."—*John Bull.*
"This is a volume of plain sermons in a simple unpretending style, adapted to the comprehension of the villagers to whom they are addressed, and inculcating many useful practical lessons."—*Church of England Magazine.*

—— Sermons, chiefly Catechetical. 12mo. cloth, 5s. 6d.

"Their plainness brings them within the comprehension of the most illiterate, whilst their exposition and illustration of Gospel truth render them a medium of usefulness, which cannot be without the very best results."—*Bell's Messenger.*

Reading without Tears; or, a Pleasant Mode of Learning to Read. By the Author of "Peep of Day," &c. With numerous Woodcuts. Third Thousand. Square, cloth, 3s.

⁎ In this little work the attempt is made, by the *classification* of words, removing all perplexity, to prevent TEARS, and by a succession of *pictures*, furnishing constant entertainment, to preserve the SMILES of happy childhood while learning to read.

"That this elementary volume is the work of the authoress of the 'Peep of Day' will be a sure passport to the hearts of thousands, both parents and children. But apart from its authorship, the book itself is admirable; the arrangement, pictures, typography, and reading exercises being alike adapted to realise the idea of the title, learning to read 'without tears.' Teachers are addressed in some valuable prefatory remarks. The authoress lays great stress on the exclusion of the element of fiction from the narratives which she has introduced as lessons."—*Record.*

The Rector in Search of a Curate. Post 8vo. cloth, 9s.

Contents.—1. The Parish—2. The Curate—3. The Temporary Curate—4, 5. The Evangelicist—6. The Evangelicals—7. The Unfortunate Man—8. The Scholar—9. The Millenarian—10. The Anglo-Catholic—11. The Approved—12. The Ordination.

"A lively and entertaining book."—*Christian Observer.*
"Interesting and attractive."—*Spectator.*

RIPON, Bishop of.—Means of Grace. Lectures delivered during Lent, 1851, in St. John's Church, Clapham Rise. By the Right Rev. ROBERT BICKERSTETH, D.D. Lord Bishop of Ripon. Fcap. cloth, 3s. 6d.

"Mr. Bickersteth's Lectures are very sterling in point of doctrinal teaching and practical enforcement."—*Christian Times.*
"These are plain, unaffected, and sensible discourses, setting forth the great outlines of Christianity and urging the necessity of holiness and obedience."—*English Review.*

RUPERT'S LAND, Bishop of.—Notes of the Flood at the Red River, 1852. By DAVID ANDERSON, D.D. Lord Bishop of Rupert's Land. Fcap. cloth, 2s. 6d.

RUSSELL, Dr.—The History of Modern Europe. With an Account of the Decline and Fall of the Roman Empire; and a View of the Progress of Society, from the Rise of the Modern Kingdoms to the Peace of Paris in 1763. In a series of Letters from a Nobleman to his Son. New Edition, continued to the present time. 4 vols. 8vo. cloth, 2l. 12s.

Scenes in our Parish. By a Country Parson's Daughter. 2 vols. 12mo. boards, each 5s.

SCOTT, Rev. T.—Essays on the most Important Subjects in Religion. By the Rev. THOMAS SCOTT, late Rector of Aston Sandford, Bucks. With a Memoir of the Author. Fifteenth Edition. 12mo. 5s.; 18mo. 3s. 6d.

Scripture Catechism; extracted chiefly from the Rev. Edward Bickersteth's "Scripture Help." Designed to assist the Young in acquiring a Knowledge of the Holy Bible, and to commend it to their love. By E. W. 18mo. 1s. sewed; 1s. 6d. cloth.

Sermons and Extracts Consolatory on the Loss of Friends. Selected from the Works of the most eminent Divines. Third Edition. 8vo. cloth, 12s.

SHAKSPEARE.—The Plays of William Shakspeare, accurately printed from the Text of the Corrected Copies, a History of the Stage, and a Life of Shakspeare. By ALEXANDER CHALMERS, F.S.A. 8 vols. 8vo. 3l. 12s.; or 1 vol. 8vo. 10s. 6d.

SHERWOOD, Mrs.—The Golden Garland of Inestimable Delights. By Mrs. SHERWOOD. 12mo. cloth, 6s.

"It possesses greater reality, and even interest, than some more ambitious-looking tales; everything in 'the Golden Garland' bears the stamp of truth."—*Spectator.*
"It serves as a vehicle to inculcate the soundest moral precepts," &c.—*Herald.*

—— The Mirror of Maidens in the Days of Good Queen Bess. 12mo. cloth, 6s.

—— The History of John Marten. A Sequel to "The Life of Henry Milner." 12mo. cloth, 7s. 6d.

—— The History of Henry Milner. 3 vols. 12mo. cloth, each 6s.

—— The History of the Fairchild Family; or, The Child's Manual. Nineteenth Edition. 3 vols. 12mo. cloth, each 5s.

—— Julietta di Lavenza. A Tale. 18mo. cl. 2s.

—— Victoria. 12mo. boards, 4s.

—— The Little Momiere. 12mo. cloth, 2s.

SHIRLEY, Bishop.—Letters and Memoir of the late WALTER AUGUSTUS SHIRLEY, D.D. Lord Bishop of Sodor and Man. Edited by THOMAS HILL, B.D. Archdeacon of Derby. Second Edition, revised. With a Portrait, 8vo. cloth, 14s.

—— Sermons preached on Various Occasions. 12mo. cloth, 6s.

"A direct plainness of style and purpose, which had the effect of force, and a sound Protestant feeling."—*Spectator.*

—— Letters to Young People. By the late Right Rev. WALTER AUGUSTUS, Bishop of Sodor and Man. Fcap. cloth, 3s. 6d.

"The volume consists of letters chiefly addressed to his son and daughter; and exhibits the writer in a very amiable, affectionate, pious, and sensible light. Some of the epistles to his son contain judicious advice on study and critical remarks on books."—*Spectator.*

"We like the general tone of these letters much. They are cheerful, unaffected, kindly, without overweening conceit or laborious condescension. They refer, too, to real incidents and events."—*Athenæum.*

SIMEON, Rev. C.—Memoirs of the Rev. CHARLES SIMEON, M.A. late Senior Fellow of King's College, and Minister of Trinity Church, Cambridge; containing his Autobiography, together with Selections from his Writings and Correspondence. Edited by the Rev. WILLIAM CARUS, M.A. Canon of Winchester. Third Edition. 12mo. cloth, with Portrait and Facsimile, 5s.

SMITH, Rev. T. D. S.—Life: an Enquiry into the Source, Actings, and Results of the Divine or Spiritual Life. By the Rev. THOS. D. S. SMITH, B.A. Curate of Bishopstoke. Crown 8vo. cloth, 6s.

SMITH, Rev. W. M.—Help to District Visitors. Being Plain and Practical Remarks on some Portions of the Gospels; particularly the Narratives and Parables. With an Appendix of Prayers selected from the Liturgy. By the Rev. W. MAXWELL SMITH, Rector of Lufton, and Perpetual Curate of Tintinhull, Somersetshire. Fcap. 8vo. cloth, 3s. 6d.

"Plain, scriptural, and affectionate, it cannot fail to do good,'whether read by those that visit the poor, or placed in village or parochial libraries."—CLERICAL JOURNAL.

"The pieces are short, sensible, and scriptural."—CHURCH OF ENGLAND MAGAZINE.

"These addresses are models of their kind."—MORNING HERALD.

"Many important topics are herein brought home to the simplest mind. The district visitor cannot do better than provide himself with the work."—BEACON.

"We shall be glad to hear that Mr. Smith's valuable work has a large circulation."—WESTERN FLYING POST.

Solace of a Mourner. Fcap. cloth, 4s. 6d.

STEPHEN, Sir G.—Anti-Slavery Recollections: in a Series of Letters addressed to Mrs. BEECHER STOWE. Written by Sir GEORGE STEPHEN, at her Request. Fcap. cloth, 4s.

STEWART, Rev. J. H.—Memoir of the Life of the Rev. James Haldane Stewart, M.A. late Rector of Limpsfield, Surrey. By his Son, the Rev. DAVID DALE STEWART, M.A. Incumbent of All Saints', Maidstone. With a Portrait. Second Edition. 12mo. cloth, 5s.

—— The Family which Jesus Loved; or the History of Martha, and Mary, and Lazarus. In Seventeen Lectures. By the late Rev. J. H. STEWART. Third Edition. Fcap. cloth, 5s.

STOKES, Rev. E.—Sermons by Edward Stokes, M.A. Student of Christ Church, Rector of Staines, late Whitehall Preacher, and Select Preacher in the University of Oxford. Fcap. cloth, 5s. 6d.

"One great advantage of English sermons over those of most foreign preachers—we speak of good specimens of either class—is, that the former will bear reading as well as hearing. Those now before us, by Mr. Stokes, illustrate this good quality; they do not deal with any controverted subject, and very little with doctrine at all; but there is a tone of real piety and of love towards Christ pervading them, which stamp them as essentially Christian sermons."—*Literary Churchman*.

STOWELL, Rev. H.—Tractarianism Tested by Holy Scripture and the Church of England, in a Series of Sermons. By HUGH STOWELL, M.A. Incumbent of Christ Church, Salford, Honorary Canon of Chester, and Rural Dean. 2 vols. 12mo. cloth, each 6s.

N.B. The object of this work is not merely nor mainly to confute Tractarianism, but rather to inform and establish the minds of Churchmen on certain perplexing questions, respecting which definite views are much needed.

—— A Model for Men of Business; or, Lectures on the Character of Nehemiah. Third Edition. Crown 8vo. cloth, 5s.

THORNTON, H.—Female Characters. By the late HENRY THORNTON, Esq. M.P. With Prayers adapted to the Lectures. Second Edition. Fcap. cloth, 3s.

—— Family Commentary on Portions of the Pentateuch; in Lectures, with Prayers adapted to the Subjects. Second Edition. Thick 8vo. cloth, 12s.

THORNTON, H.

—— On the Ten Commandments, with Prayers.
Second Edition. 12mo. cloth, 2s. 6d.

—— Family Prayers, in a Series for a Month.
Thirty-sixth Edition. 12mo. cloth, 3s.

—— Family Commentary upon the Sermon on the Mount. Second Edition. Fcap. cloth, 3s.

TRACTS for Distribution.

The Angel's Message; or, the Saviour made known to the Cottager. By the Author of "Peep of Day." Third Thousand. Square 16mo. price 6d.

Also, by the same Author,

Teaching Myself; or, an Abridgment of "Reading without Tears." For the Cottager in his own Home. Third Thousand. Square 16mo. price 6d.

By the same Author,

Tracts for Children; or, Fifty-two Facts from the Bible for the Fifty-two Sundays of the Year. Thirteenth Thousand. In a packet of Fifty-two Tracts; or, bound together in a volume, cloth gilt, price 2s.

The German Tree. A Moral for the Young. By the Rev. T. GOODWIN HATCHARD, M.A. Rector of Havant, Domestic Chaplain to the Marquis Conyngham. 1s.

By the same Author,

Feed My Lambs. A Lecture for Children in Words of One Syllable; to which is added a Hymn. Seventh Thousand. 32mo. 3d.; or 2s. 6d. per dozen.

My Duty. The Christian Duties, taken from the Church Catechism, printed in red and black within an ornamental Gothic Tablet; intended for Parochial Distribution. 4d. each; or 3s. 6d. per dozen.

TRACTS for Distribution.

The Fourth Commandment Explained. By a Sunday-School Teacher. 3d.; or 2s. 6d. a dozen.

The Teacher's Assistant in Needle-work. 6d. each, or 5s. per dozen.

The Knitting-Teacher's Assistant. 6d.; or 5s. per dozen.

A Misfortune Changed into a Blessing. 12mo. 6d.; or 1s. cloth.

Eliezer; or, The Faithful Servant. 12mo. 3d.; or 2s. 6d. per dozen.

How can I go to Church? or, a Dialogue between a Lady and a Poor Woman. 3d. each.

Why should I not go to the Meeting-House? 3d. each.

Seed-Time and Harvest. Some Account of "Schools for the Destitute." By the Author of "The Gospel of Other Days." Third Edition. 6d.

A Friend to the Sick and Afflicted. 3d.; or 2s. 6d. per dozen.

Thoughts on the Sabbath. 12mo. 3d.

Reflections on the Sabbath. By Sir HENRY DYMOKE. 12mo. 3d.

Repairing the Church. 3d.; or 2s. 6d. per doz.

Narrative of Poll Peg, of Leicestershire. 3d.; or 2s. 6d. per dozen.

TRACTS for Distribution.

The Curate Catechising; or, an Exposition of the Church Catechism. By the Rev. W. Thistlethwaite, A.M. Sixth Edition. 18mo. 1s.

By the same Author,

The Church Communicating; or, an Exposition of the Communion Service of the Church of England. 18mo. 6d.

The Parochial Minister's Letter to the Young People of his Charge on Confirmation. By the Rev. John Langley, Rector of St. Mary's, Wallingford. 12mo. 2s. per dozen.

A Short Catechism; or, Plain Instruction, containing the Sum of Christian Learning, set forth by the authority of his Majesty, King Edward the Sixth, for all Schoolmasters to Teach, A.D. 1553. 18mo. 6d.; or 5s. per dozen.

Confirmation: its Nature, Importance, and Benefits. By the Rev. T. Griffith, A.M. 4d.; or 3s. 6d. per dozen.

A Plain and Affectionate Address to Young Persons about to be Confirmed. By the Right Rev. D. Wilson, late Lord Bishop of Calcutta. 12mo. 4d.

By the same Author,

A Plain and Affectionate Address to Young Persons, previously to Receiving the Lord's Supper. 12mo. 4s.

TUPPER, M. F.—Proverbial Philosophy. By Martin F. Tupper, D.C.L. &c. Post 8vo. cloth, with Portrait, 8s.

—— An Illustrated Edition of Proverbial Philosophy.

The Designs by

C. W. Cope, R.A.
Fred. R. Pickersgill, A.R.A.
John Tenniel.
Edward H. Corbould.
George Dodgson.
Edward Duncan.
Birket Foster.

John Gilbert.
James Godwin.
William Harvey.
J. C. Horsley.
William L. Leitch.
Joseph Severn.
Walter Severn.

The Ornamental Initials and Vignettes by Henry Noel Humphreys.

In 4to. bound in cloth, gilt edges, 1l. 11s. 6d.; morocco, 2l. 8s.; morocco by Hayday, 2l. 12s. 6d.

TUPPER, M. F.

—— The Pocket Edition of Proverbial Philosophy. Thirty-fourth. 16mo. cloth, gilt leaves, 5s.

—— Probabilities: an Aid to Faith. Third Edition. Fcap. cloth, 4s.

"It is difficult to convey, by extracts, the charm which is diffused over this little book. There is, in the infinite variety of subject, a continuous line of thought, which fixes the attention to its progress, and leaves the mind amused and edified with the perusal."—*Christian Remembrancer.*

TYTLER, Miss A. F.—Leila; or, the Island. Eighth Edition. Fcap. 8vo. cloth, 4s. 6d.

—— Leila in England. A Continuation of "Leila; or, the Island." Sixth Edition. Fcap. cloth, 6s.

—— Leila at Home; a Continuation of "Leila in England." By ANN FRASER TYTLER. Fourth Edition. Fcap. 8vo. cloth, 4s. 6d.

"'Leila at Home,' in continuation of 'Leila in England,' is written in the same pleasant style, and conveys similar lessons of an instructive and religious tendency."—*Literary Gazette.*

—— Mary and Florence; or, Grave and Gay. Eleventh Edition. Fcap. cloth, 4s. 6d.

—— Mary and Florence at Sixteen. Fifth Edition. Fcap. cloth, 6s.

"These works are excellent. Miss Tytler's writings are especially valuable for their religious spirit. She has taken a just position between the Rationalism of the last generation and the Puritanism of the present, while the perfect nature and true art with which she sketches from juvenile life, show powers which might be more ambitiously displayed, but cannot be better bestowed."—*Quarterly Review.*

TYTLER, Miss M. F.—The Wooden Walls of Old England: or, Lives of Celebrated Admirals. By MARGARET FRASER TYTLER. Containing Biographies of Lord Rodney, Earls Howe and St. Vincent, Lords de Saumarez and Collingwood, Sir Sydney Smith and Viscount Exmouth. Fcap. cloth, 5s.

—— Tales of the Great and Brave. Containing Memoirs of Wallace, Bruce, the Black Prince, Joan of Arc, Richard Cœur de Lion, Prince Charles Edward Stuart, Nelson, and Napoleon Bonaparte. Second Edition. Fcap. cloth, 5s.

VENN, Rev. H.—Memoir and Selection from the Correspondence of the Rev. H. Venn, M.A. Edited by the Rev. Henry Venn, B.D. Prebendary of St. Paul's. Seventh Edition. Fcap. cloth, 7s.

Verschoyle. A Roman Catholic Tale of the Nineteenth Century. 12mo. cloth, 6s.

VICTORIA, Bishop of.—Lewchew and the Lewchewans; being a Narrative of a Visit to Lewchew, or Loo-Choo, in October, 1850. By George Smith, D.D. Bishop of Victoria. Fcap. cloth, 2s. 6d.

—— Hints for the Times; or, the Religions of Sentiment, of Form, and of Feeling, contrasted with Vital Godliness. Fcap. sewed, 1s. 6d.

"A sensible and seasonable little treatise."—*Christian Guardian.*

WEBB, Mrs. J. B.—The Beloved Disciple. Reflections on the History of St. John. By Mrs. J. B. Webb, Author of "Naomi," "Reflections on the History of Noah," &c. Fcap. 8vo. cloth, 4s. 6d.

"Very sensible and well-written reflections on the History of St. John. We can safely recommend it."—*Christian Guardian.*

WHITE, Rev. G.—The Natural History and Antiquities of Selborne. By the Rev. Gilbert White, M.A. A New Edition, with Notes, by Edward Turner Bennett, Esq. F.L.S. &c. 8vo. cloth, 18s.

WILLYAMS, Miss J. L.—Chillon; or, Protestants of the Sixteenth Century. An Historical Tale. By Jane Louisa Willyams. 2 vols. 8vo. cloth, 10s.

"We think highly of this pathetic story. A true spirit of cheerful piety pervades its pages; the characters are nicely discriminated, and many of the scenes are very vividly portrayed. All who read it may derive benefit from its perusal."—*Britannia.*

WOLFE, Rev. C.—Six Plain Sermons, preached to a Rural Congregation. By the Rev. CHARLES WOLFE, late Curate of Kemsing, Kent. Fcap. cloth, 2s. 6d.

WOODWARD, Rev. H.—Short Readings for Family Prayers, Essays, and Sermons. By the Rev. HENRY WOODWARD, A.M., formerly of Corpus Christi College, Oxford; Rector of Fethard, in the Diocese of Cashel. 8vo. cloth, 12s.

Words of Wisdom for my Child; being a Text for Every Day in the Year, for the use of very Young Children. Second Edition. 32mo. cloth, 2s.

YORKE, Rev. C. J.—Original Researches in the Word of God. By the Rev. C. J. YORKE, M.A. Rector of Shenfield. Fcap. cloth, 5s.

    I. Christ Known before His Advent.
    II. The Beauty of the Mosaic Law.
    III. Inspiration and Genius.
    IV. The Divine Recognition of the Spiritual Church.
    V. The Development of Pure Religion.
    VI. The Apostolic Motive.
    VII. God Apparent in His Miracles and Prophecies.
    VIII. Scriptural Imagery: its Uses, Marks, and Sources.
    IX. God Traced in the World, and Found in Christ.
    X. The Human Conscience.

www.ingramcontent.com/pod-product-compliance
Lightning Source LLC
Chambersburg PA
CBHW030019240426
43672CB00007B/1018